From zero to Grade 2 in 75 minutes!

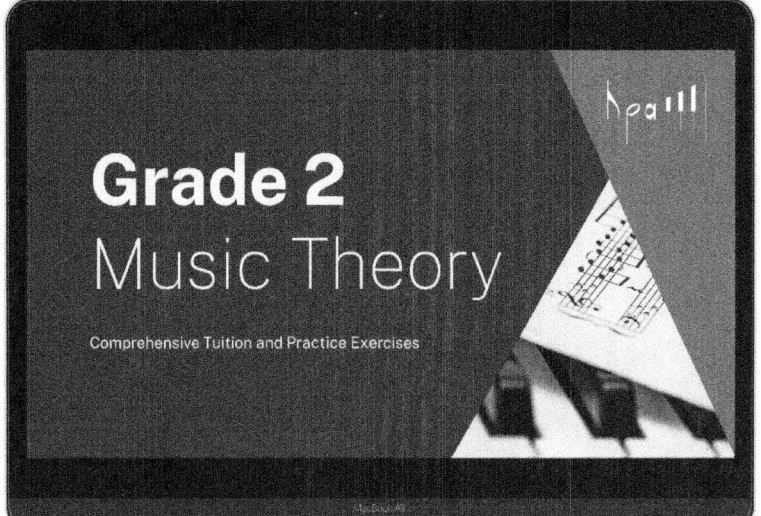

Video Course

hampsteadpianoacademy.com

Copyright © 2022 Hampstead Piano Academy

All rights reserved.

No portion of this book may be reproduced in any form without permission from the publisher, except as permitted by U.S. copyright law. For permissions contact: info@hampsteadpianoacademy.com

Index

Contents

Index

Introduction

Notation

    The Music Stave

    The Grand Stave

    Parts of a Note

    Writing Notes

        Drawing note-heads or semibreves

        Drawing stems

        Drawing tails

Clefs

    The Treble Clef

    The Bass Clef

    Writing changes of clefs

    Pitch

    Ledger Lines

Time Values

    Note Values

    Rest Values

Drawing rests
Music Note Tree
Dotted Values
Drawing Dots
Dotted rests values
Bars and bar lines
Ties and slurs
Lengthening weak beats
Accidentals on tied notes

Time Signatures
What are the numbers for?
Time Signatures Classification
Common time and Alla breve
Time signatures accentuation
Changes of time signatures

Confusing time signatures
Rewriting music in a new time signature
From 4/4 to 4/2
From 3/4 to 3/8
From 3/2 to 3/4
From 2/2 to 2/4

Triplets
How to write triplets

Grouping Notes

Beaming foundation
- Notes with the same number of flags
- Notes with different number of flags
- Dotted notes

Time signatures with a crotchet beat
- Beaming Quavers
- Beaming Semiquavers
- Beaming Dotted Rhythms
- Avoid ties
- Syncopation
- Rests in 2/4, 3/4, 4/4

Time signatures with a minim beat
- Beaming quavers and semiquavers in 2/2, 3/2, 4/2
- Rests in 2/2, 3/2, 4/2
- Avoid ties

Time signatures with a quaver beat
- Beaming quavers and semiquavers in 3/8
- Rests in 3/8

Grouping Rests – General rules
- Whole Bar Rest
- Grouping rests shorter than a beat

Accidentals
- Writing an accidental
- Cancelling an accidental

Keys and Key Signatures
- Major and minor modes
- Grade 2 Key Signatures
- Writing Key Signatures
- The Circle of Fifths
- How to find the Major key of a Key Signature
- How to find the key signature of a minor key
- How to find the key of a piece

Scales
- Tones and Semitones
- Major Scales
  - Grade 2 Major scales
  - Descending Major Scales
- Degrees
- Minor scales
  - Grade 2 minor scales

Chords
- Tonic Triad
- Chord inversions
- Arpeggios
  - Broken chords

Intervals
- Harmonic and Melodic
- Measuring Intervals by number

              Intervals and Accidentals
              Unison and Octave
              Grade 2 Intervals
       Measuring intervals by quality
              Major and minor 2^{nds}
              Major and minor 3^{rds}
              Perfect 4^{ths}
              Perfect 5^{ths}
              Octaves (8^{ves})

Ostinato

       Sequences

Transposition

Performance Directions

       Dynamics

       Tempo

              Tempo Markings

              Tempo Changes

              Metronome Marks

       Articulation

              Legato

              Staccato

              Accent

              Tenuto

              Sforzando

- Marcato
- Legato-staccato
- Staccatissimo

Repeat Marks
- Repeat Signs
- First and second time bar
- Da Capo al Fine
- Dal Segno

Expression Terms
- Cantabile
- Dolce
- Espressivo
- Giocoso
- Grazioso
- Maestoso

Other signs and terms
- Octave
- Fermata
- Other terms
- Musical Vocabulary

Introduction

In Grade 2, you will learn the fundamentals of music notation, basic key signatures, scales, chords and intervals. Some musical terms, signs and their meaning.

During the course, you will also apply all concepts into practical exercises and actual extracts of music. You will learn how to understand and appreciate the detailed composers' writing so your performances are more musical and meaningful.

Let's get started!

Notation

Music notation is the system of symbols used to write music. It is a language on its own which allows performers to translate the elements of music and communicate them through sounds.

The first element of notation we will introduce is the music stave.

The Music Stave

The stave (or staff) is the system of five parallel horizontal lines and four spaces where the notes are written on.

```
5 ─────────────────────────────────
   4
4 ─────────────────────────────────
   3
3 ─────────────────────────────────
   2
2 ─────────────────────────────────
   1
1 ─────────────────────────────────
```

Musical notes can be written either on the lines or in the spaces.

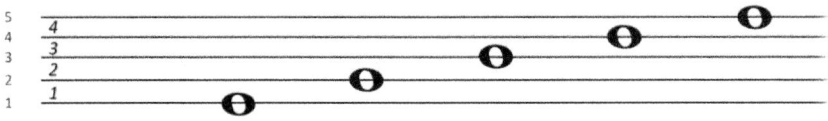

The Grand Stave

Piano and some other instruments music are written on the Grand Stave: a pair of two staves joined together one above the other by a brace. The brace shows that the music represented on the two staves should be played simultaneously. We will continue with the notes.

Parts o f a Note

The parts of a note are:

The Note-head
it is simply an oval.

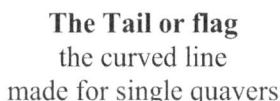

The Stem
the line coming from the note-head.

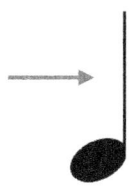

The Tail or flag
the curved line
made for single quavers

The Beam
the top line that joins two or
more quavers or semiquavers

13

Writing Notes

Drawing note-heads or semibreves

If a note-head or semibreve is drawn on a line, the line must go exactly through the middle. If it is drawn in a space, the oval should fill the space.

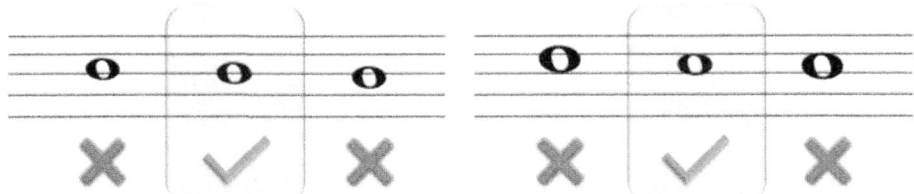

Drawing stems

Notes below the middle line should have their stems pointing upwards and notes above the middle line should have their stems pointing downwards. For the third line itself, both directions are correct.

When drawing a stem, remember that upward stems should come from the right side of the note-head and downward stems should be on the left side of the note-head. Last but not least, stems should be written vertically and should not be too short or too long.

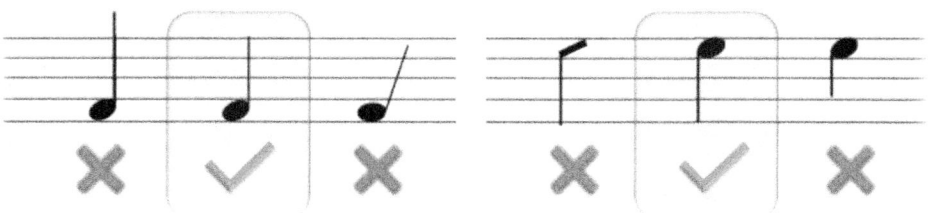

Drawing tails

Tails are always drawn on the right side of the stem, regardless of the direction the stem points.

Clefs

In order to represent pitch in the stave, a clef should be written. There are many different clefs but, in this level, you only need to learn the treble clef and the bass clef.

Together with a clef, a stave indicates the pitch of a musical note.

But… what do we mean by pitch? The pitch of a note is basically how high or low the sound is. For example, all these notes are C but each of

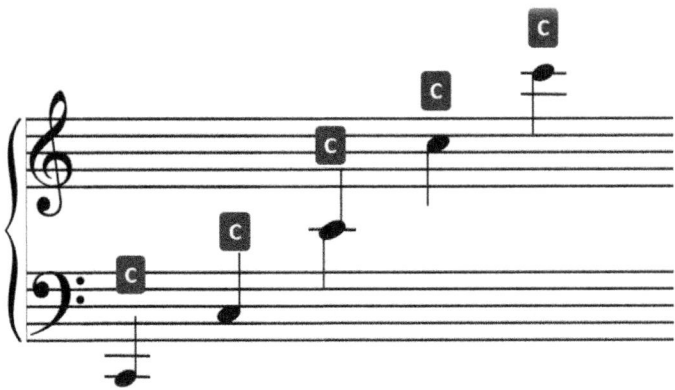

them has a different sound.

Clefs must be written on every stave, not just the first one, and always at the beginning: before the key and time signatures

The Treble Clef

The treble clef is also known as the "G" clef, because the middle part of it is always looped around the second line. So, when you draw it, you should always start with a dot on the second line. Then make a snail-shaped curve that touches the third and first line and continue all the way above the fifth line. Last step, just draw a vertical line that passes through the first dot you made and finish with a little turn.

The Bass Clef

In order to represent lower sounds, a different clef is needed: the bass clef. It is much easier to draw as it looks like the right-side of a heart shape. The bass clef is also known as "F" clef, because the two dots placed above and below the fourth line, represent F.

When drawing this clef, we also need to make sure the spot where to begin drawing the heart is the fourth line. Otherwise, if heart and dots are in another place, we will be drawing a completely different clef.

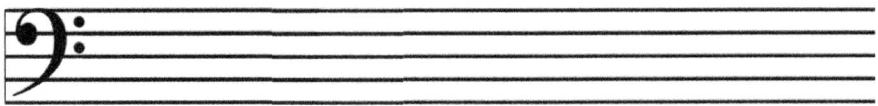

Writing changes of clefs

Clefs may be changed at any point to facilitate sight reading. We just need to pay attention to write them properly in these circumstances:

- When it occurs in the middle of the bar, it is simply written

where needed.

- If the change of clef happens from a bar to the next, the clef should be written **before the bar-line**.

- If the change applies to the start of a new line, the clef should also be shown at the **end of the previous line,** just as a warning.

Pitch

The pitch of a note is basically how high or low the sound is.

Pitch notation is a sophisticated system, especially when different clefs are combined. However, it is always useful to imagine a piano keyboard to learn the musical notes that can be found in a grand stave.

Notes are drawn either on the lines or in the spaces to represent different sounds. In English, the name of the notes follows the alphabet: A, B, C, D, E, F, G.

Middle C is a good point to start learning the notes. It takes this name for being in the centre of the piano keyboard and for being in the middle range of the human voice tessitura. It is also the C between the two staves in a Grand Stave.

As the stave is filled up with notes on the lines and in the spaces, a considerable range of sounds can be symbolised.

If we need to represent pitches higher or lower than these in the stave, we need ledger lines. (Notes marked in yellow below).

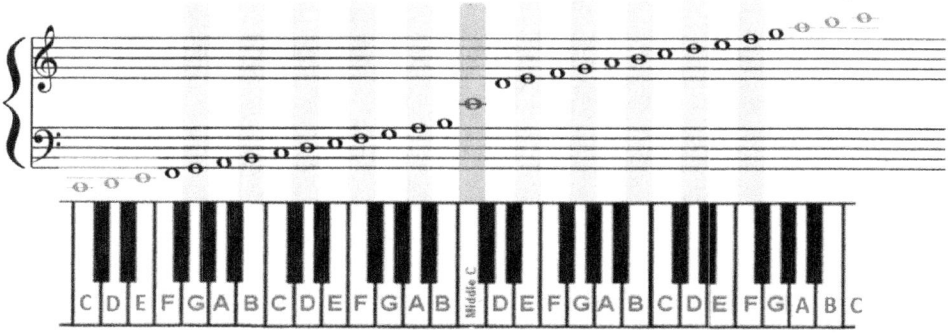

Ledger Lines

Ledger lines are short lines placed above or below the stave to represent higher or lower sounds. They act as an extension of the stave.

When drawing them, the distance between the ledger lines should be the same distance as in between each of the lines on the stave. They must be straight and should not slope up or down. On the other hand, we should not confuse the notes on the ledger lines in bass and treble clefs, as they may have similar shapes but they are not the same notes.

By the way! The line that middle C has is a ledger line!

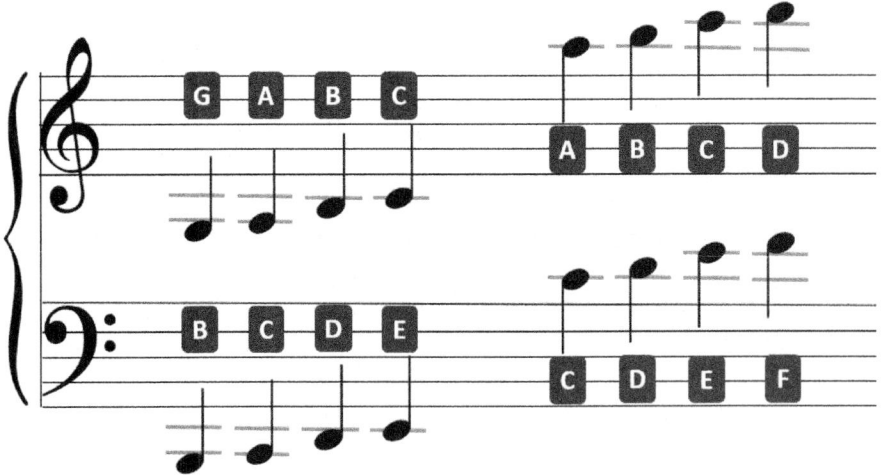

Attention! Place ledger lines accidentals carefully so that they belong to the correct notes.

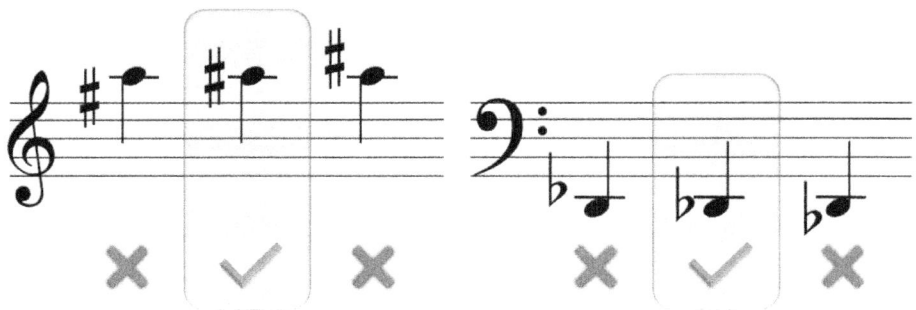

To continue with, we will introduce the basics of rhythm.

Pitch

https://forms.gle/wjnqa8Aju4SwjsR6A

Time Values

Music is the art of combining sounds in time. Therefore, it requires a system to define how long each sound is in order to be organized in time.

Note Values

The duration of a sound is called time value or note value. Depending on how long a sound is, it can be represented with different signs.

Let's start with the **semibreve**. Or if you are in the States, you may call it whole note. It is simply written as an oval and it lasts for four beats.

If a stem is put on it, it halves the length of the note. We make it a **minim** (or half note) and the duration is two beats.

To continue with the next, we just colour the note-head in.
This one is called **crotchet** (or quarter note) and it is worth one beat.

After that, we can get even shorter values. If a tail is added to the note, it forms a **quaver** and its duration is half beat.
In the American nomenclature, it is called eighth note.

When there are two tails, the note is worth a quarter of a beat.
Its name is **semiquaver** or sixteenth note.

Rest Values

Music is a combination of sound and silence. Depending on how long the silence is, it can be represented with different signs. You have already learned how to represent the duration of a sound. Let's have a look to the way silence can be written:

Each note has a rest of the same duration.

The **semibreve rest** looks like a little box that hangs from the fourth line of the stave.
It can also be called whole rest and it lasts for four beats.

It's important to watch the difference between the semibreve rest and the **minim rest**.
They look similar but the minim rest sits on the third line.
A minim rest lasts for two beats and it is also known as half rest.

Minim mounted

Then, there is the **crotchet or quarter rest**, which is worth one beat.

Shorter rests have the same number of tails as the notes with the same duration.
This will be the **quaver or eighth rest**, worth half of a beat.

And the **semiquaver or sixteenth rest**, is worth a quarter of a beat.

Drawing rests

Semibreve rest   *Minim rest*

Semibreve and minim rests are easy to be drawn. You just need to make sure the little boxes touch the correct line.

To draw a crotchet rest, break it into two parts.

For the quaver rest, the little circle should always be drawn in the third space, regardless of the pitch of the note.

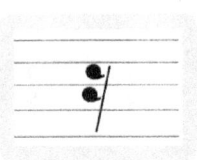

The semiquaver rest, would have two little circles: one in the third space and another one in the second space, regardless of the pitch of the note.

Remember that all rest tails are always drawn on the right side.

Music Note Tree

All time values we have learned so far are relative to each other. Each figure is worth twice as much, or half as much, as the next one.

In other words:

- A semibreve is as long as two minims.
- A minim is as long as two crotchets.
- A crotchet is as long as two quavers
- And a quaver is as long as two semiquavers.

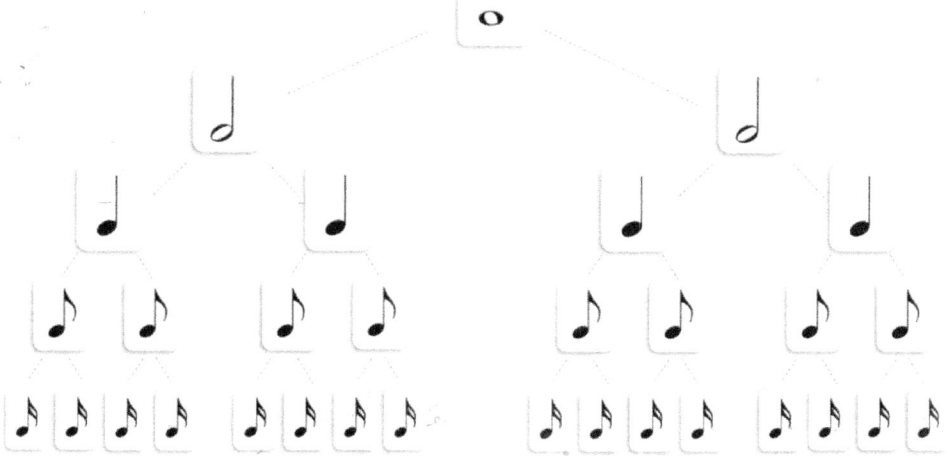

Or we can also say that:

A semibreve equals the sum of two minims, or four crotchets, or eight quavers or sixteen semiquavers.

Dotted Values

When a dot is put on the right side of a note, its duration is augmented. A dot after a note makes it half as long again.

Let's see how a dot affects a semibreve:

There are four beats in a semibreve. What is the half of four? Two. And two is the value of a minim. So, a dotted semibreve equals the sum of a semibreve plus a minim.
It lasts for a total of **6 beats** and can also be called **dotted whole note.** It may not look too familiar but from this grade, you will see them more often.

To find out the length of a **dotted minim** (or dotted half note) the same process applies:
There are two beats in a minim. What is the half of two? One. And one is the value of a crotchet.
So, a dotted minim equals the sum of a minim plus a crotchet. It lasts for a total of **3 beats**.

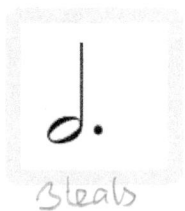

After these, we will be talking about shorter values.

A crotchet is worth one beat. And the half of one is actually half. What is the note value that lasts for half a beat? The quaver.
So, a **dotted crotchet** equals the sum of a crotchet plus a quaver and it lasts for a total of **one and a half beats**.
It is also known as dotted quarter note.

To continue with **dotted quavers** or dotted eighth notes, we should not panic. A quaver lasts for half beat. What is the half of a half? A quarter. And a quarter is the value of a semiquaver.
So, a dotted quaver equals the sum of a quaver plus a semiquaver. It lasts for a total of **three quarters of a beat**.
It can also be called dotted eighth note.

Drawing Dots

Dots are written at the right side of the note or rest. If the note-head is in a space, the dot goes in the same space. If the note-head is on a line, the dot is drawn in the space just above the line. Dots are never written on the lines because they are not easy to see.

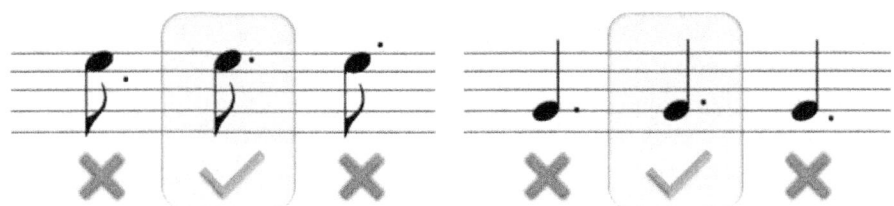

On the other hand, augmentation dots should not be confused with staccato dots. Staccato dots are always written below or above the head note and augmentation dots go always on the right side.

Dotted rests values

The same way that a dot affects the duration of a note, it can also lengthen the value of a rest.

The rule is the same: **a dot after a rest makes it half as long again**.

Consequently, the **dotted minim rest** or dotted half rest equals a minim rest and a crotchet rest and it lasts for 3 beats.

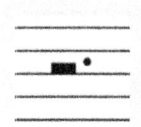

The dotted crotchet rest or dotted quarter rest equals a crotchet rest plus a quaver rest and it is worth a beat and a half.

The dotted quaver rest or dotted eighth rest is the sum of a quaver rest plus a semiquaver rest and equals three quarters of a beat.

It is important to watch that in any form of dotted rest, the dot is **written in the third space**.

Bars and bar lines *Same as book 3*

All the note and rest values we have learned so far, need to be organised in time. This is the reason why classical music writing has time signatures, bars and bar lines.

Beats are organized into bars, with a bar line at the end of each one. Watch out that the last bar line of a piece is double and thicker to indicate the end.

Bars can hold many types and number of beats but in Grade 1, we will only explain bars holding two, three or four crotchet beats. We will talk about time signatures in the next chapter.

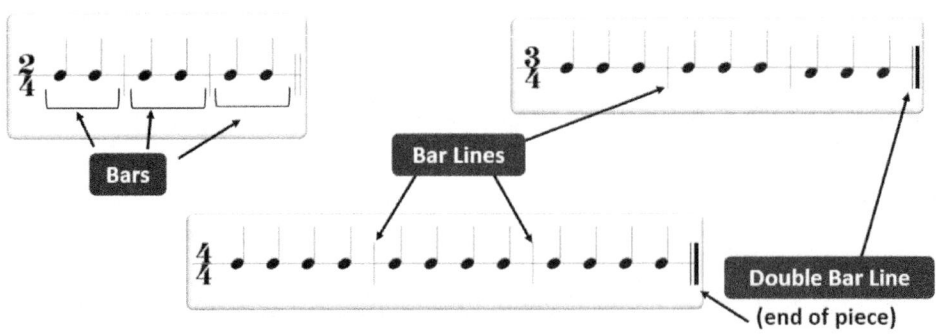

Ties and slurs *Same as book 3*

A tie is a curved line which connects notes of exactly the same pitch. Its function is to join two or more notes to make one single longer sound. Ties should not be confused with slurs.

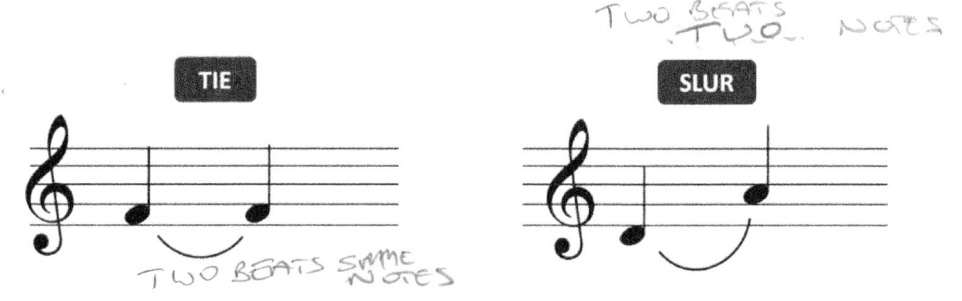

TWO BEATS TWO NOTES

TIE　　　　　　　　　　**SLUR**

TWO BEATS SAME NOTES

Slurs are also curved lines but they are used on different notes to represent smooth playing between them.

Ties can be drawn across bar lines and can join any number of notes. These notes must be the same pitch and they must be next to each other. Ties go from the head of the first note to the head of the next and should be written on the opposite side of the stem.

There are two ways that notes can be altered to make them longer. The first way is adding a dot to it, as explained in the previous chapter, and the other way is using a tie.

Ties are applied in two occasions: when the note needs to be held across a bar line or when the added-on part of the note falls on a strong beat. This concept will be explained in the "Time Signatures Accentuation" chapter.

Let's have a look to ties across a bar line:

To write a sound that lasts, for example, six beats in a 3/4 time signature, a tie is needed to connect two dotted minims and add up 3 + 3.

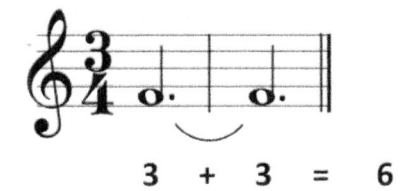

3 + 3 = 6

Here is another example to write a sound that lasts for six beats as well but now in a 2/4 time signature. We simply have to draw another tie to join three minims together and count 2 + 2 + 2.

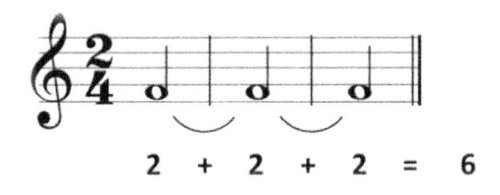

2 + 2 + 2 = 6

And in a 4/4, it will be a minim tied to a semibreve. 2 + 4 beats.

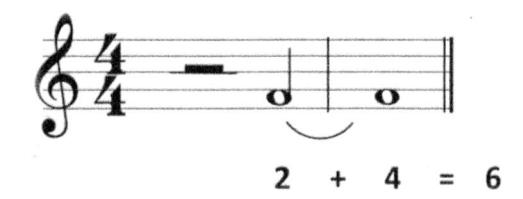

2 + 4 = 6

Lengthening weak beats

The other occasion when a tie may be used instead of a dotted note needs more attention.

As a general rule, dotted notes must not be written to lengthen a note from a weak beat into a strong beat. Instead, ties should be used. There is more information about strong and weak beats in the "Time Signatures Accentuation" chapter.

For example, in a 4/4 time signature, the second beat is weaker than the third and should not be crossed by a dot.

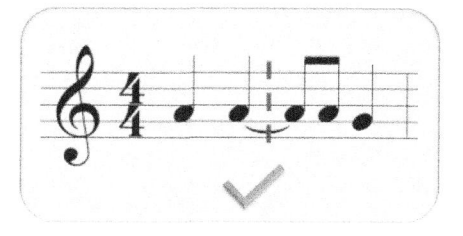

Accidentals on tied notes

If an accidental is applied to tied notes, it will continue to affect the held note, even across bar lines.

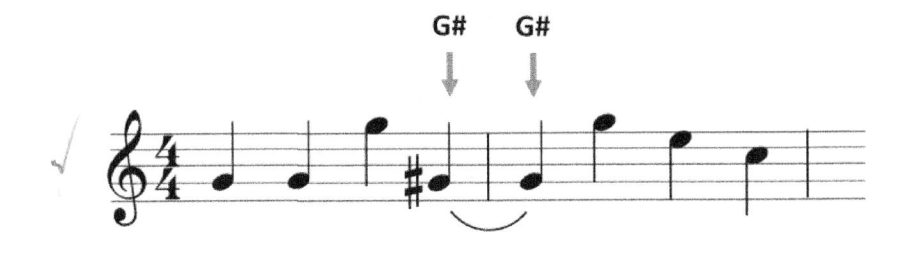

If the harmony changes during a long tied note and the same sound is represented in a different way, (in other words, enharmonized), the note should continue to be held.

Attention! Sometimes, tied notes are carried over to the next line of music.

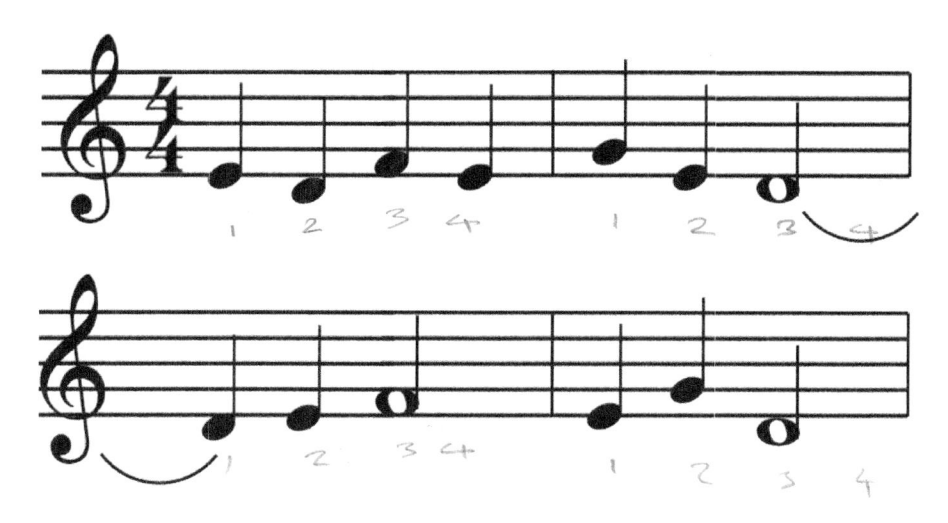

Last but not least, rests are never tied. The silence just continues:

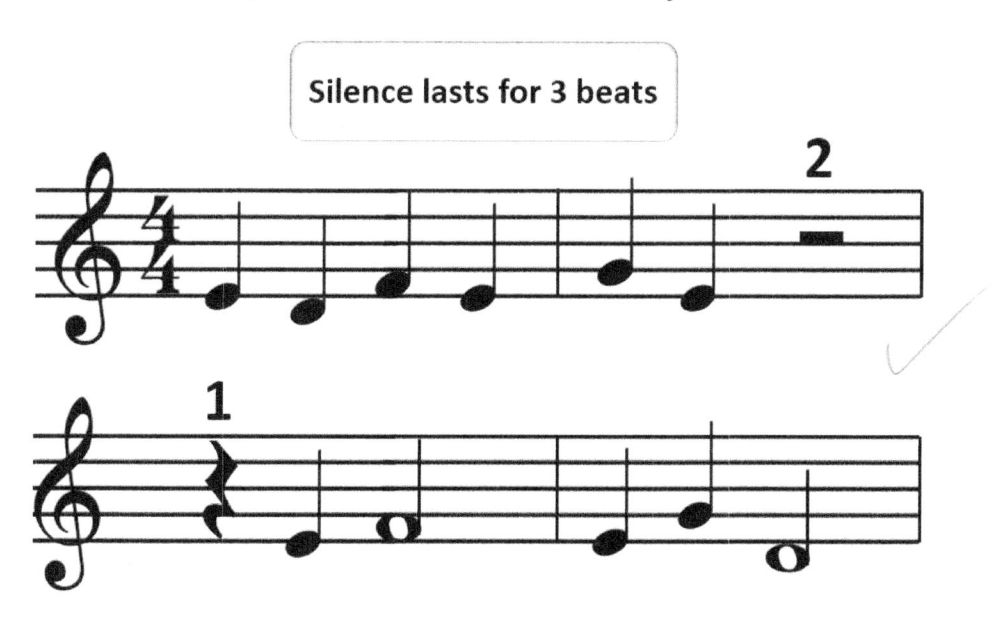

Silence lasts for 3 beats

Time Signatures

The time signature is a pair of two numbers aligned vertically that organizes music in time. It defines the amount and the type of beats contained in a bar.

It is also known as meter signature or measure signature.

What are the numbers for?

Time signatures can be classified in two ways:

- by the number of beats in a bar (top number)

- by the kind of note used to represent the beat (bottom number)

$\frac{2}{4}$ — BY NUMBER OF BEATS

— BY TYPE OF BEATS

Time Signatures Classification

The classification by number of beats in a bar is the easiest:

→ **Duple time**: When there are two beats in a bar
→ **Triple time**: When there are three beats in a bar
→ **Quadruple time**: When there are four beats in a bar.

The classification by type of beats may not be so straightforward.

→ Starting with the most basic, **number 4** represents that the beat is a **crotchet**.
→ **Number 2** represents that the beat is a **minim**.
→ And **number 8** represents that the beat is a **quaver**.

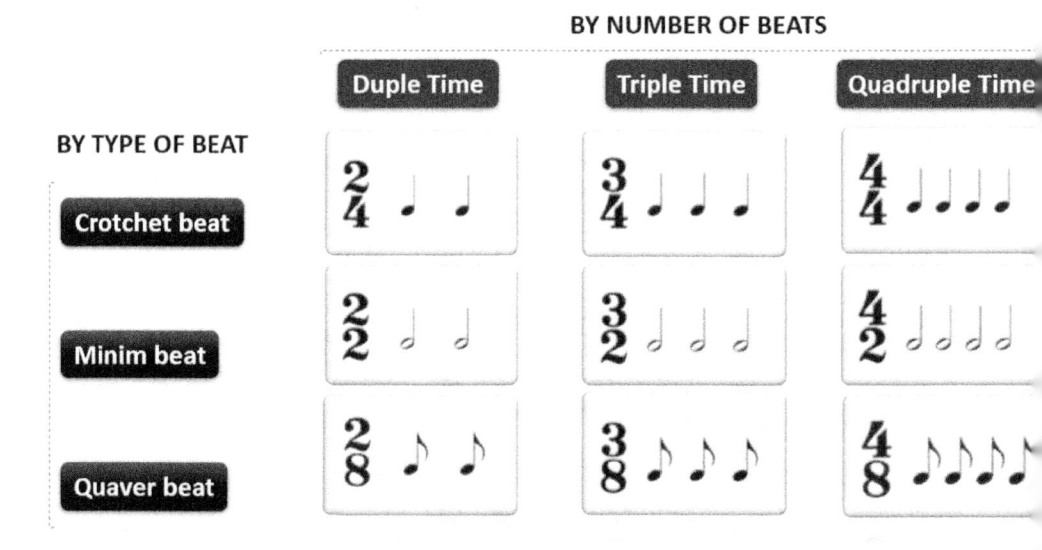

	Duple Time	Triple Time	Quadruple Time
Crotchet beat	2/4 ♩ ♩	3/4 ♩ ♩ ♩	4/4 ♩ ♩ ♩ ♩
Minim beat	2/2 ♩ ♩	3/2 ♩ ♩ ♩	4/2 ♩ ♩ ♩ ♩
Quaver beat	2/8 ♪ ♪	3/8 ♪ ♪ ♪	4/8 ♪ ♪ ♪ ♪

BY NUMBER OF BEATS (columns) / BY TYPE OF BEAT (rows)

Common time and Alla breve

Time signatures are not always written with numbers.

4/4 can also be represented as **C**. This is known as **Common Time** and it has the same meaning as a 4/4 time signature.

2/2 can also be represented as **¢**. This is called **Alla Breve** and it has the same meaning as a 2/2 time signature.

Time signatures accentuation

All time signatures have a hierarchy of strong and weak beats. The first beat of every bar should be slightly emphasized, although never hammered!

This little accentuation means that not all the beats sound the same and it adds a particular character to the music.

The natural accentuation in a duple time signature, is strong-weak. Or, to give you a clearer idea, we could think of forte-piano.

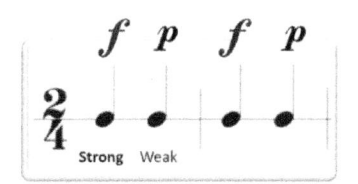

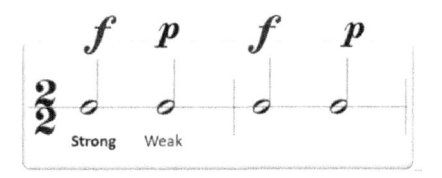

→ In a triple time signature, the normal accentuation would be strong-weak-weak.

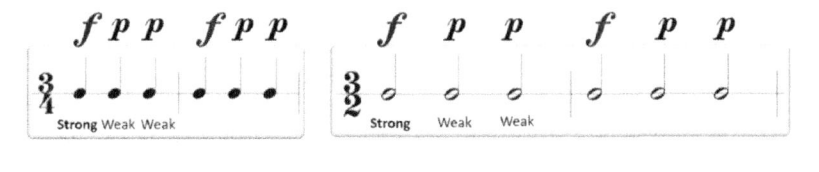

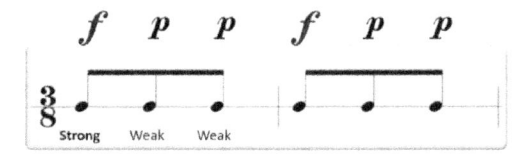

→ In a quadruple time signature, there will be a strong-weak pair of beats followed by another "less strong-weak" two.

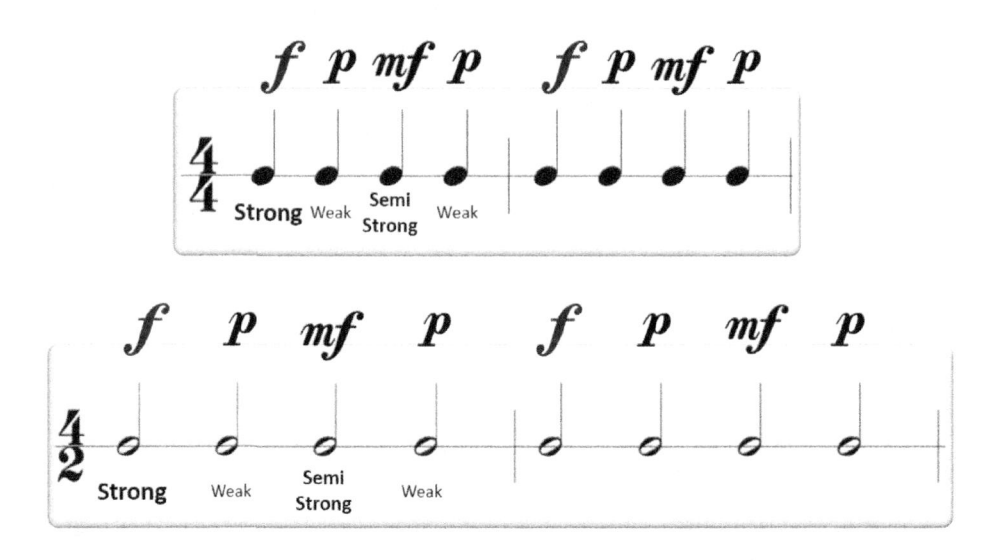

However, this is just a guide to show you how some beats are more important than others within a bar, and it does not mean you need to strictly perform your music following these dynamics.

Changes of time signatures

The time signature appears at the beginning of the piece, after the clef and the key signature, but it can also be changed throughout the piece.

We just need to remember that changes of time signatures always come

after the bar-line.

If the change applies to the start of a new line, the new time signature should also be shown at the **end of the previous line**, just as a warning.

Confusing time signatures

Let's first have a look at the numbers in the key signatures.

They are going to give us all the information we need.

The top number tells us how many beats we have in each bar or measure.

And the bottom number tells us which kind of beat is used.

NUMBER OF BEATS → 2
KIND OF BEATS → 2

4/4

Okay! So, when two is the upper number, we will have two beats in a bar.

And when four is the upper number, there will be four beats in a bar.

NUMBER OF BEATS → 2/2 ←   4/4 ←

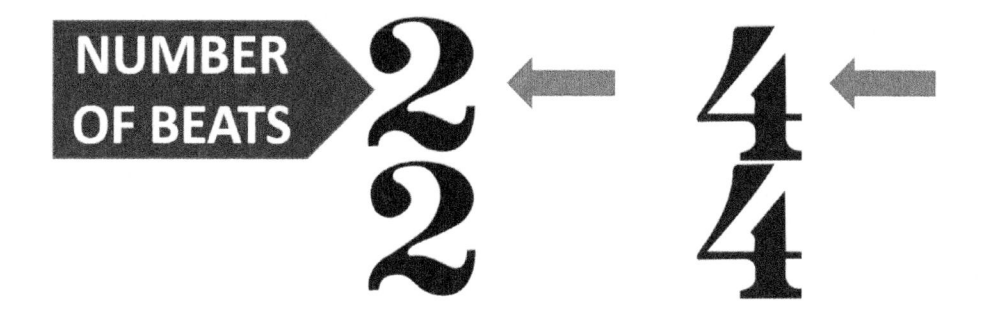

Alright that seems easy! Let's look now at the bottom number.

Remember that the lower number tells us which kind of beat we have. And here is where all the mystery is!

The two at the bottom tells us we have minim beats (half note beats).

And when there is a four at the bottom, that's telling us we have crotchet beats.

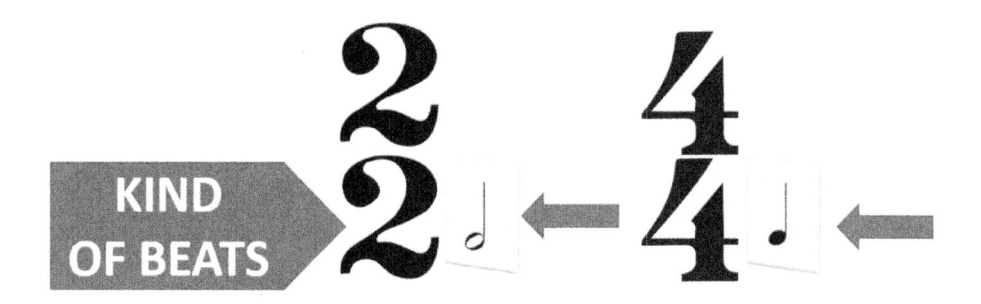

KIND OF BEATS → 2/2 ♩ ←   4/4 ♩ ←

So, in a 2/2 time signature we have 2 minim beats in a bar.

And in a 4/4 time signature we have 4 crotchet beats in a bar.

But, isn't it the same thing?...

We could easily fit 4 crotchets or 2 minims in both a 2/2 and a 4/4 time signature. Then, what's the difference?

Well, mathematically, both time signatures may look the same on paper but they feel different musically.

The top number is giving us here the information we need. Because the key to the problem is actually the number of beats.

While we have 4 beats on a 4/4, we only have 2 beats on a 2/2.

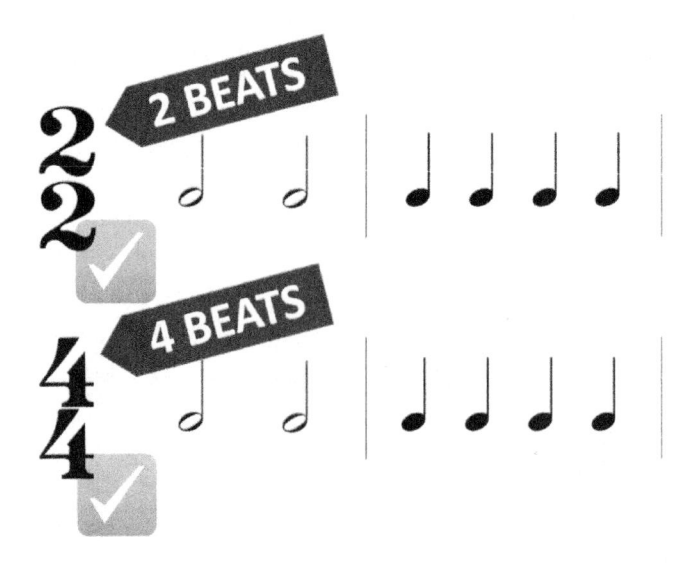

So, for example, let's think of a piece in 4/4 that, by the way, we could also write it as C or common time.

If I play a piece of music in 4/4, I will need to feel four beats in a bar. One, two, three, four. One, two, three, four.

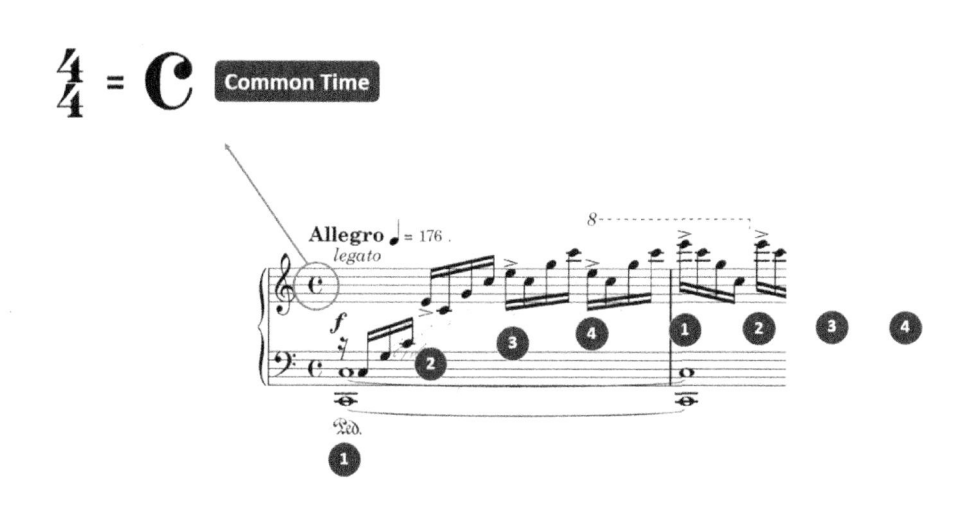

$\frac{4}{4}$ = **C** `Common Time`

Remember that we are not going to feel the same emphasis on all beats. The first beat is normally the strongest of the bar. And the fourth beat, the weakest.

Let's now have a look to a piece in 2/2. In this case, we could also write it as alla breve or cut common time. When we put a straight line through the C, what we are doing is halving the numbers.

So, if we play a piece of music in 2/2, we will feel only two beats in a bar.

One, two. One, two.

Difference between $\frac{4}{4}$ + $\frac{2}{2}$ *time*

That is the difference! We feel 4 beats on a 4/4 while we only feel 2 beats on a 2/2.

But why would we want to do this? Well, in terms of writing, music written in 2/2 works better at a faster speed.

But it is not only a question of speed! It is something composers work out and has to do with the character of the music.

Does this music sound in two-time or four-time?

So, now we know this is not a mathematical difference, because mathematically they're the same. It really is a musical difference!

Rewriting music in a new time signature

These extracts are written in a **different** way, but they sound exactly the **same**:

As a consequence, sometimes it may be easier to interpret an extract of music in a new time signature.

Now, we are going to learn how to represent some extracts of music in different time signatures:

From 4/4 to 4/2

First of all, remember that in 4/4, there are four **crotchet** beats in a bar. However, in 4/2, there are also four beats, but those are **minims beats**. When "translating" a rhythm from one time signature to the other, we should shorten or lengthen the value of each note.

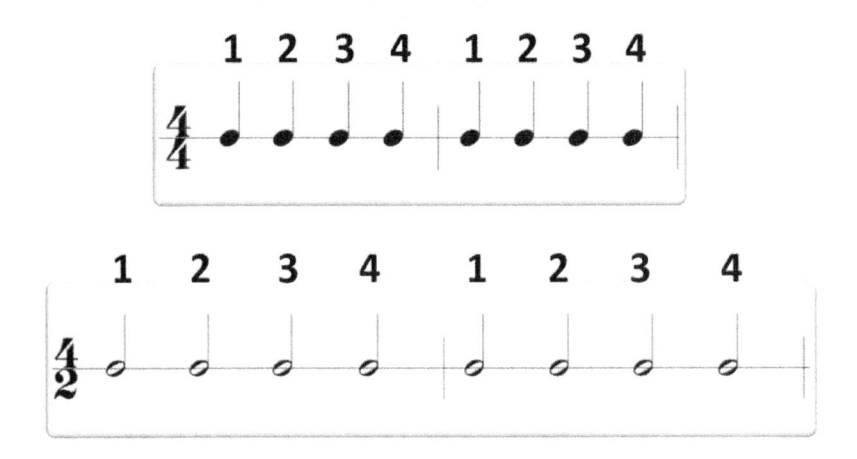

Let's look at this example to rewrite from 4/4 to 4/2:

The first note in 4/4 is a crotchet, and we know that fills one beat. What is the value that fills one beat in 4/2? The minim. My first note in 4/2 should then be a minim.

To continue with the second beat, ask yourself the same question: in 4/2, how can I fill one beat with two notes? The answer is two crotchets.

If we carry on rewriting, we find a minim in 4/4. That lasts for two beats. What value can I write to fill two beats in 4/2? A semibreve.
We got to the end of the first bar so let's double check we have four minim beats.

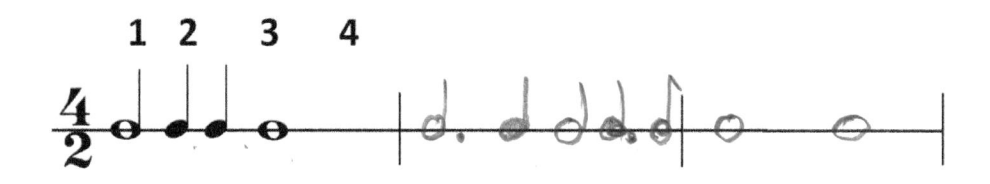

The golden rule, is that to switch from 4/4 to 4/2, I should double the value of each note. This way, all minims in 4/4 will become semibreves in 4/2, crotchets will be minims, quavers will be crotchets and so on so forth. Even rests or dotted values will be doubled.

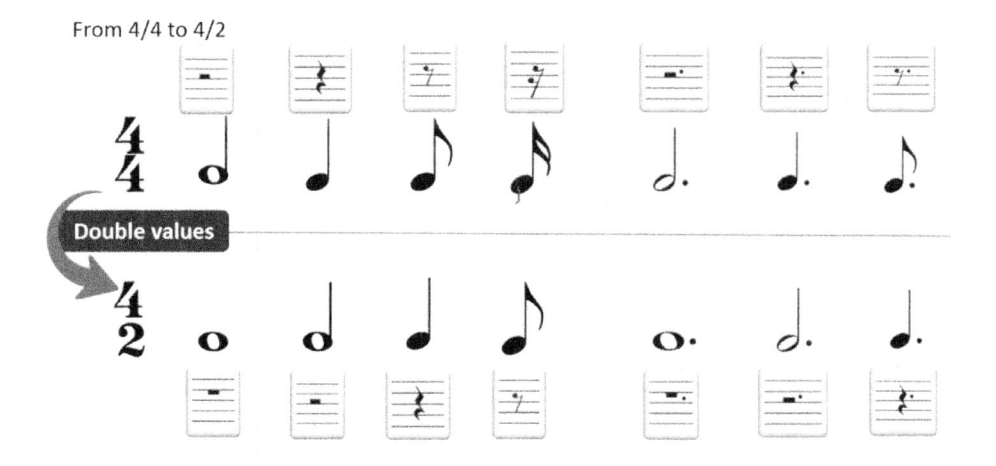

Hence, our previous 4/4 exercise would look like this if we rewrite it in 4/2:

If we want to make the opposite operation and "translate" an **extract of music from 4/2 to 4/4,** the trick is to **half the value of each note**:

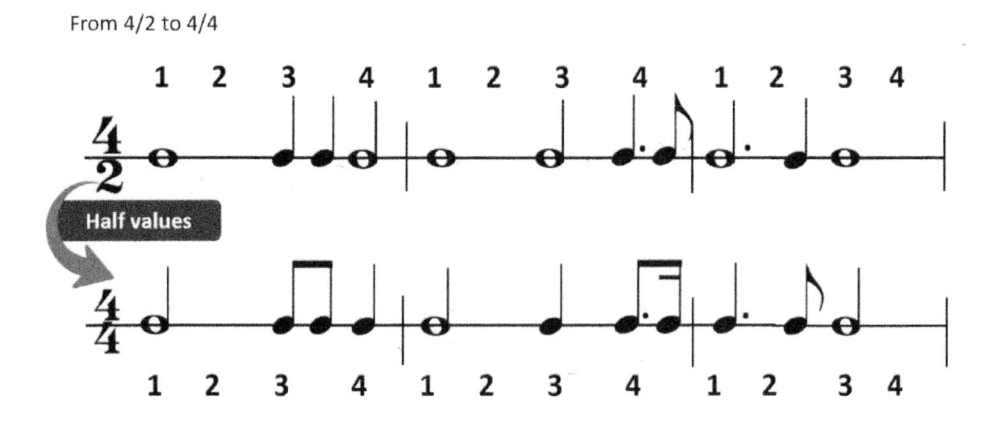

From 3/4 to 3/8

Always before starting writing, remind yourself of the number and type of beats you will be using.

In 3/4, there are three **crotchet** beats in a bar. However, in 3/8, there are also three beats, but they are **quavers.** When switching a rhythm from one time signature to the other, the golden rule of shortening or lengthening the value of each note also applies.

Let's look at this example to rewrite from 3/4 to 3/8:

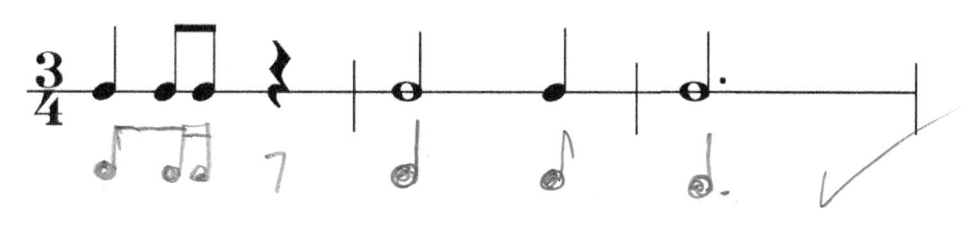

The first note in 3/4 is a crotchet, and we know that fills one beat. What is the value that fills one beat in 3/8? The quaver. My first note in 3/8 should then be a quaver.

To continue with the second beat, ask yourself the same question: in 3/8, how can I fill one beat with two notes? The answer is two semiquavers.

If we carry on rewriting, we find a crotchet rest in 3/4. That lasts for one beat. What value can I write to fill one silent beat in 3/8? A quaver rest.

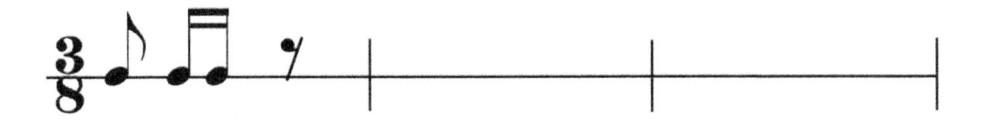

Now, pay attention to the **beaming rules** in the new time signature, as a quaver followed by two semiquavers, should be grouped together under the same beam. More information about this subject can be found in the "Grouping notes" chapter.

We got to the end of the first bar so let's double check we have three quaver beats:

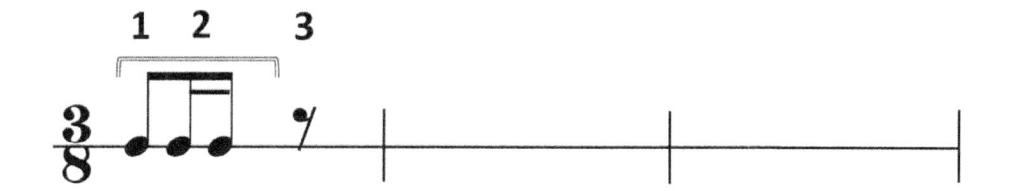

The secret is that, **to switch from 3/4 to 3/8, I should half the value of each note.** This way, all minims in 3/4 will become crotchets in 3/8, crotchets will be quavers, quavers will be semiquavers and so on so forth. Even rests or dotted values will be halved.

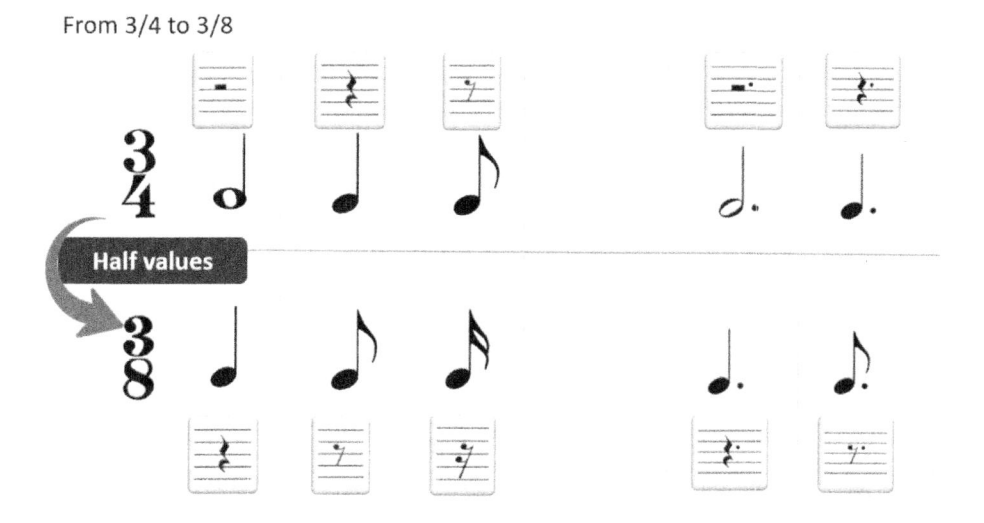

From 3/4 to 3/8

Hence, our previous 3/4 exercise would look like this if we rewrite it in 3/8:

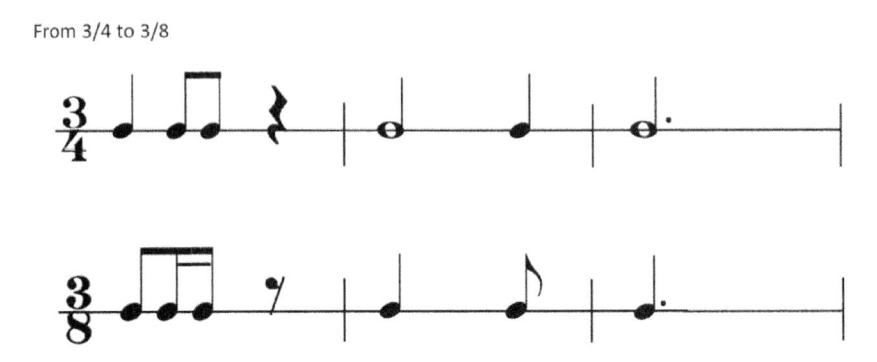

From 3/4 to 3/8

If we want to make the opposite operation and **rewrite an extract of music from 3/8 to 3/4**, the trick is to **double the value of each note**:

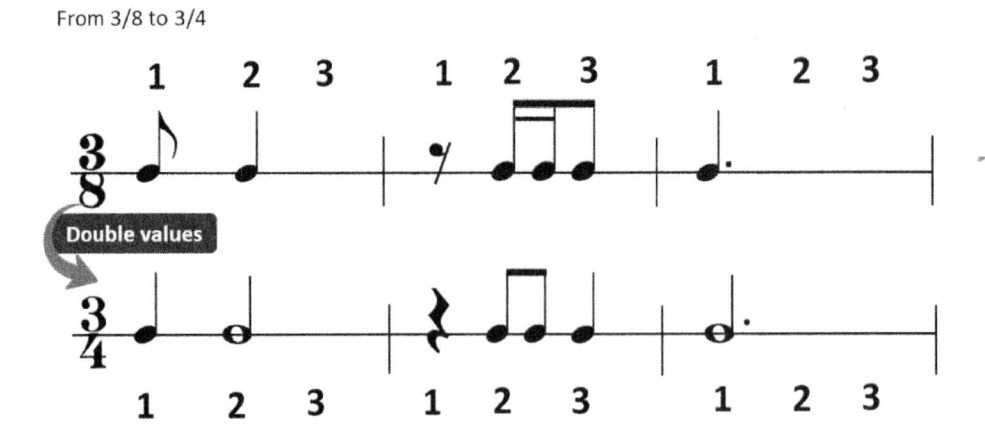

From 3/8 to 3/4

From 3/2 to 3/4

In 3/2, there are three **minim** beats in a bar. However, in 3/4, there are also three beats, but they are **crotchets.** When rewriting a rhythm from one time signature to the other, always remember the golden rule of shortening or lengthening the value of each note.

From 3/2 to 3/4

In this example, we will rewrite from 3/2 to 3/4:

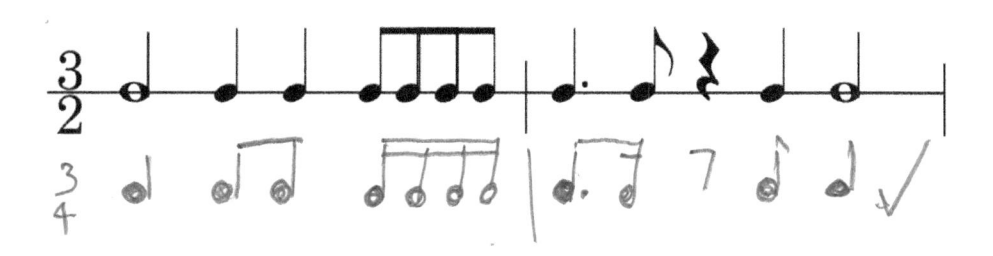

The first note in 3/2 is a minim, and we know that fills one beat. What is the value that fills one beat in 3/4? The crotchet. My first note in 3/4 should then be a crotchet.

To continue with the second beat, ask yourself the same question: in 3/4, how can I fill one beat with two notes? The answer is two quavers.

If we carry on rewriting, we find four quavers in 3/2. That occupies the space of one beat. How can I write four notes that will fill this last beat in 3/4? Don't panic: four semiquavers.

We got to the end of the first bar so let's double check we have three crotchet beats:

Remember this rule: **to switch from 3/2 to 3/4, I should half the value of each note.** This way, all minims in 3/2 will become crotchets in 3/4, crotchets will be quavers, quavers will be semiquavers and so on so forth. Even rests or dotted values will be halved.

From 3/2 to 3/4

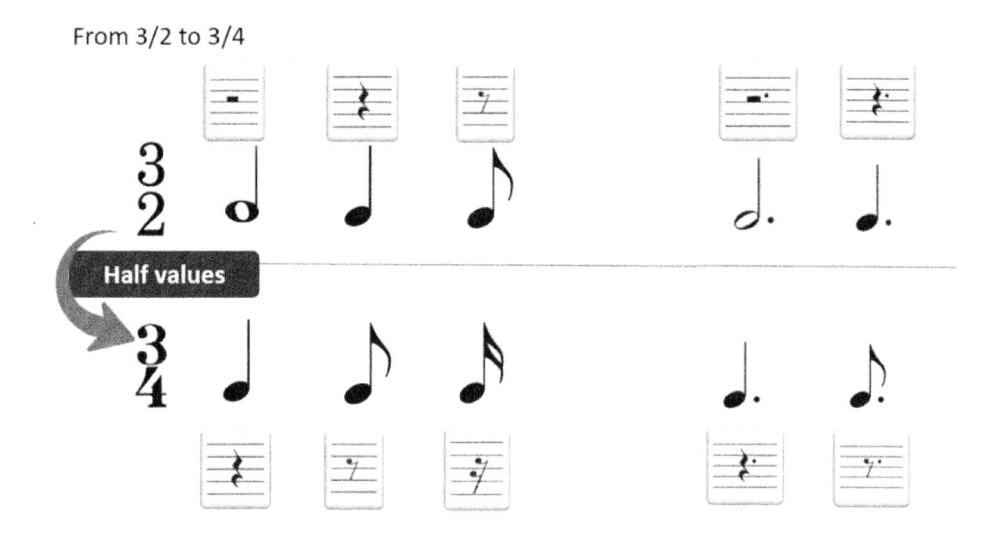

Hence, our previous 3/2 exercise would look like this if we rewrite it in 3/4:

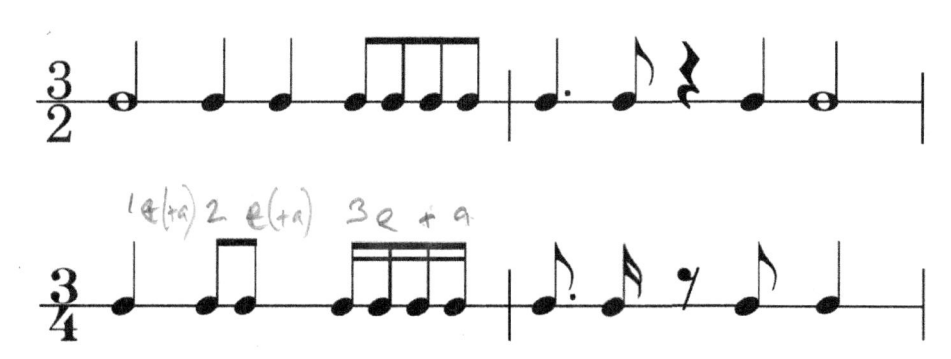

Now, pay attention to the **beaming rules** in the new time signature, as a dotted quaver followed by a semiquaver, should be grouped together under the same beam. More information about this concept can be found in the "Grouping notes" chapter.

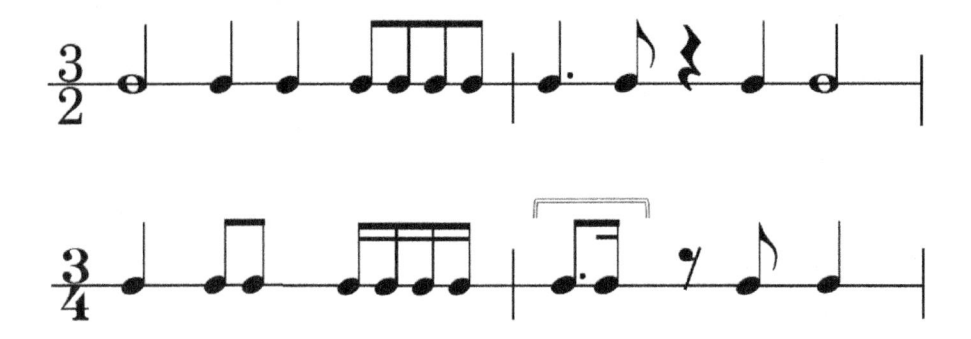

If we want to make the opposite operation and **rewrite an extract of music from 3/4 to 3/2,** the trick is to **double the value of each note:**

From 2/2 to 2/4

In 2/2, there are two **minim** beats in a bar. However, in 2/4, there are also two beats, but they are **crotchets.** When "translating" a rhythm from one time signature to the other, the golden rule of shortening or lengthening the value of each note will help you.

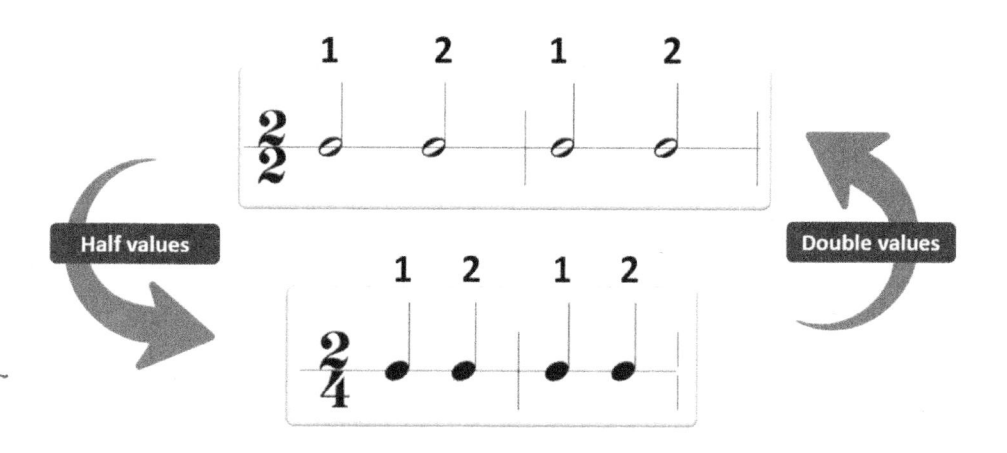

In this example, we will rewrite an excerpt from 2/2 to 2/4:

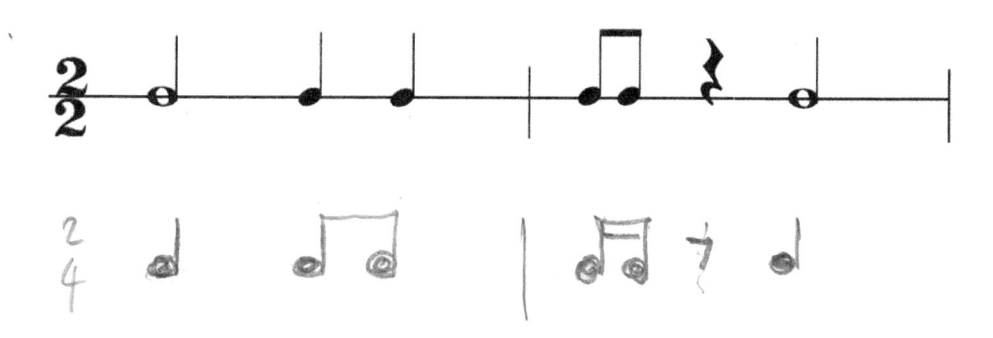

The first note in 2/2 is a minim, and we know that fills one beat. What is the value that fills one beat in 2/4? The crotchet. My first note in 2/4 should then be a crotchet.

To continue with the second beat, ask yourself the same question: in 2/4, how can I fill one beat with two notes? The answer is two quavers.

If we carry on rewriting, we find two quavers in 2/2. That occupies the space of half beat. How can I write two notes that will only fill this half beat in 2/4? Don't hesitate: two semiquavers.

Now, pay attention to the **beaming rules** in the new time signature, as quavers and semiquavers within the same beat need to be grouped together. More information about these rules can be found in the "Grouping notes" chapter.

In order to complete the remaining half, I need to find the equivalent of a crotchet beat in 2/2 to fill the other half beat in 2/4. The correct value will then be a quaver rest.

The last beat of the 2/2 is a minim and as we saw before, minims are replaced by crotchets.

Let's double check we have two crotchet beats on each bar:

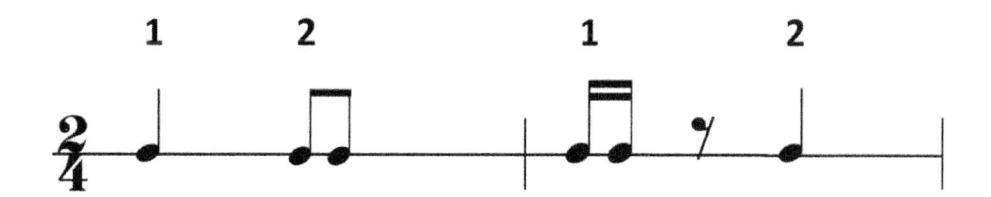

Summarizing: **to switch from 2/2 to 2/4, I should half the value of each note.** This way, all minims in 2/2 will become crotchets in 2/4, crotchets will be quavers, quavers will be semiquavers and so on so forth. Even rests or dotted values will be halved.

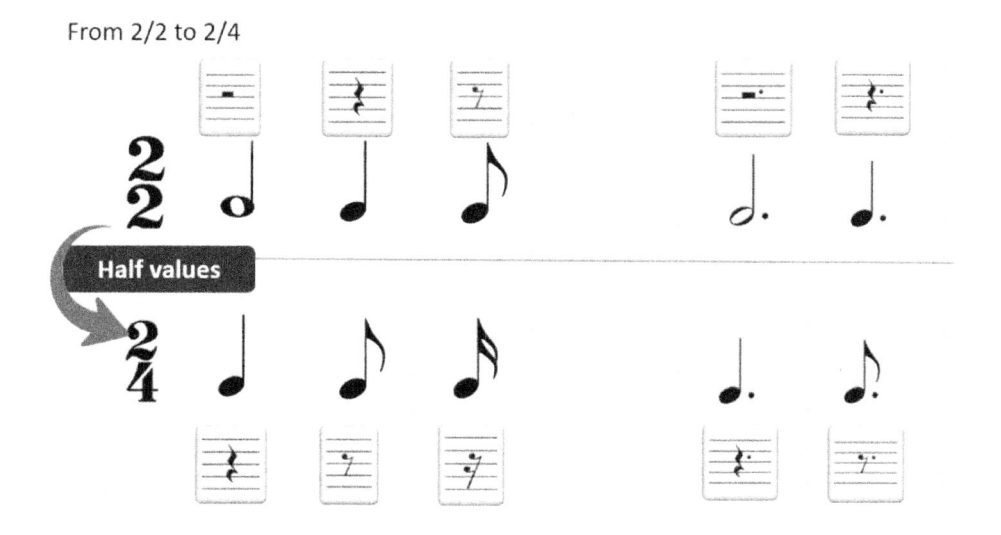

From 2/2 to 2/4

If we want to make the opposite operation and **rewrite an extract of music from 2/2 to 2/4,** the trick is to **double the value of each note:**

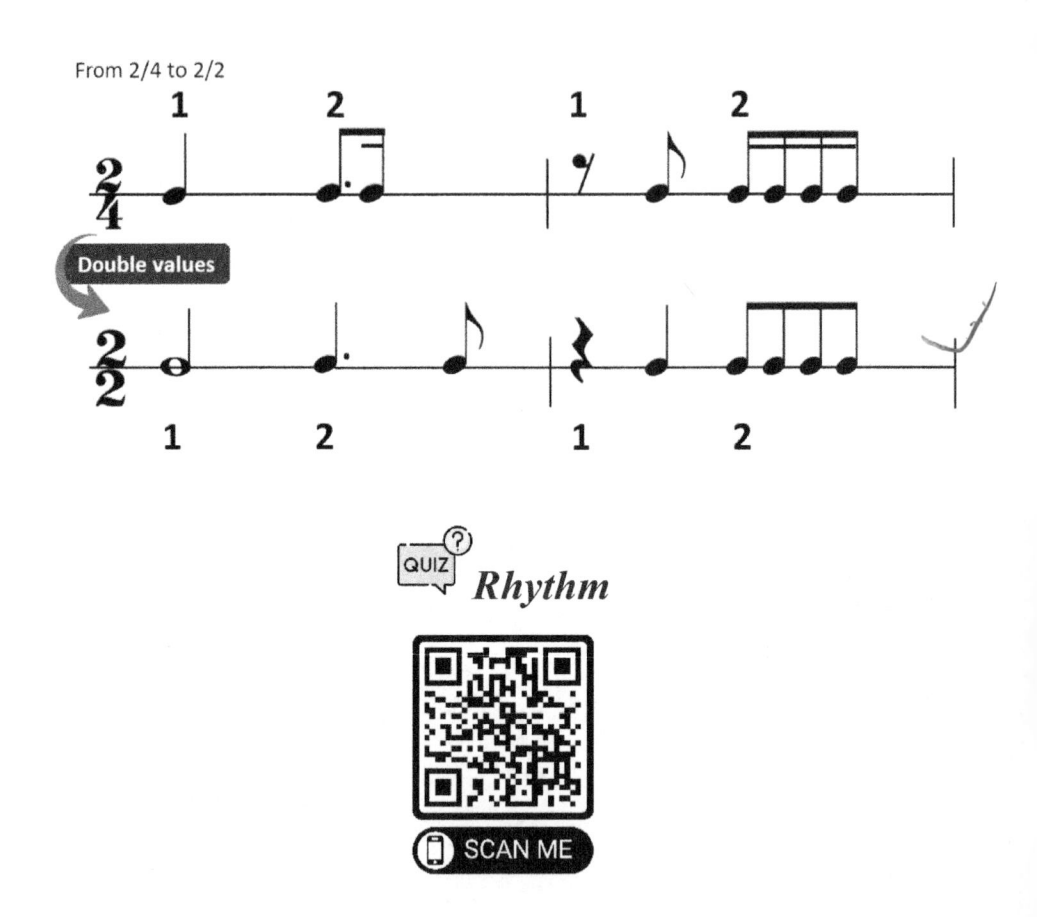

From 2/4 to 2/2

Double values

Rhythm

https://forms.gle/xWDu45vVPVqsSfmt7

"Two for the price of 1"

Triplets

A beat of any kind can be divided into two or **three equal parts**. When it is divided into three equal parts, the resulting figure is called triplet.

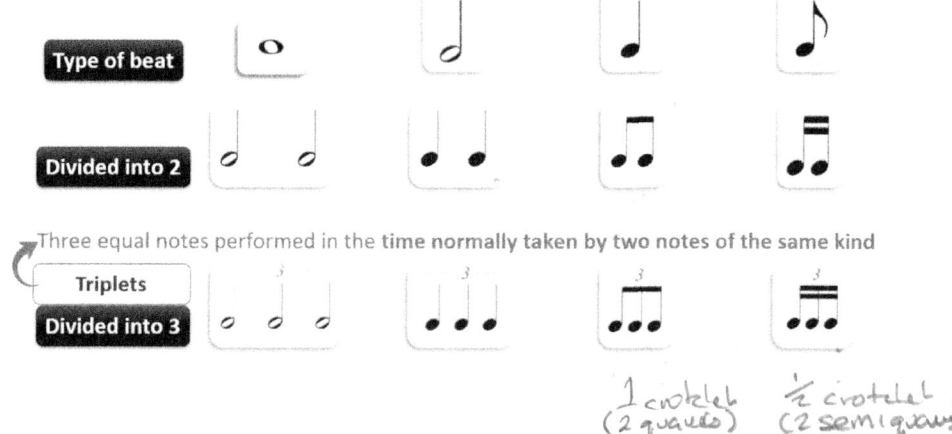

Type of beat	𝅝	𝅗𝅥	♩	♪
Divided into 2	𝅗𝅥 𝅗𝅥	♩ ♩	♫	♬
Triplets / Divided into 3	𝅗𝅥 𝅗𝅥 𝅗𝅥 (3)	♩ ♩ ♩ (3)	♫♩ (3)	♬♩ (3)

Three equal notes performed in the **time normally taken by two notes of the same kind**

1 crotchet (2 quavers)   ½ crotchet (2 semiquavers)

In other words, a triplet is a group of three equal notes performed in the **time normally taken by two notes of the same kind**. This table will help you understand triplets better:

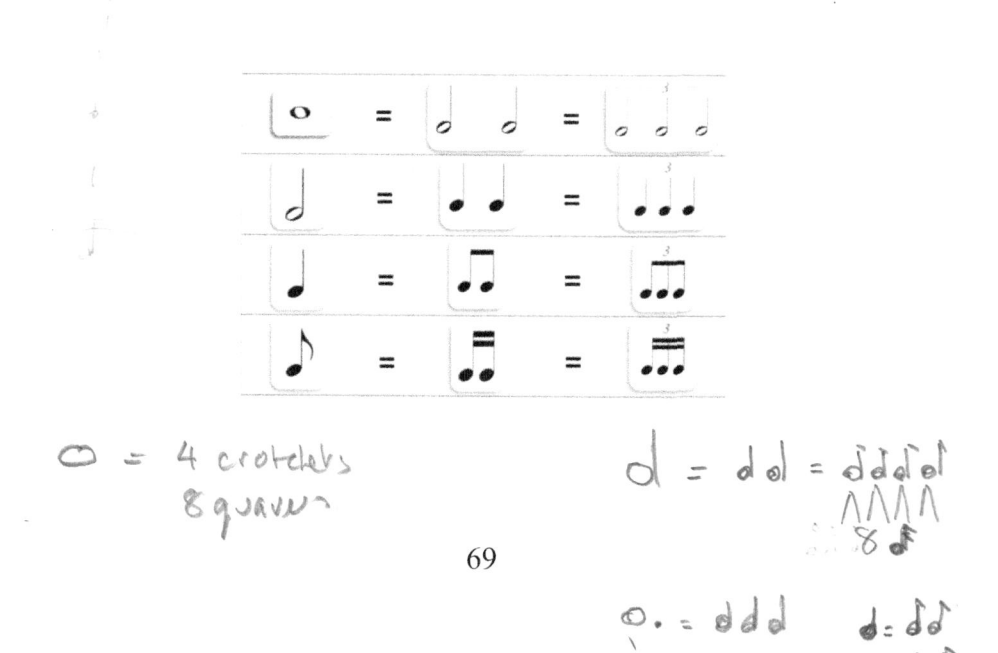

𝅝	=	𝅗𝅥 𝅗𝅥	=	𝅗𝅥 𝅗𝅥 𝅗𝅥 (3)
𝅗𝅥	=	♩ ♩	=	♩ ♩ ♩ (3)
♩	=	♫	=	♫♩ (3)
♪	=	♬	=	♬♩ (3)

𝅝 = 4 crotchets
    8 quavers

𝅗𝅥 = ♩ ♩ = ♪♪♪♪
         8 ♪

𝅝. = ♩♩♩   ♩ = ♪♪
              = 4 ♬

However, triplets can get very sophisticated to make richer rhythms:

With one or more notes becoming silent and represented as rests:

With dotted rhythms, when a note "steals" half value from the next.

How to write triplets

Triplets may have the number 3 over or under the three notes.

They can also include a curved line or bracket to distinguish them from ordinary rhythms.

Look at this to learn when to beam, write the number 3, draw a bracket **or not.**

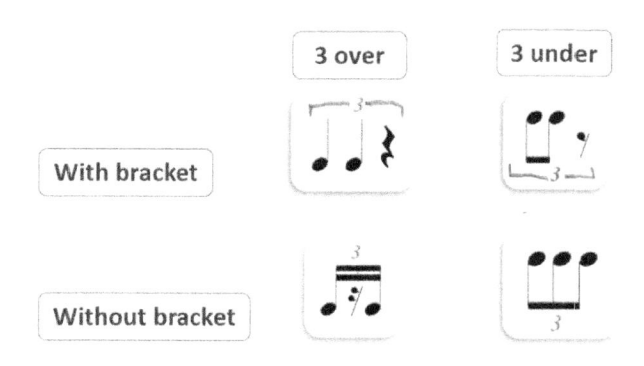

Longer notes such as **crotchets or minims need a curved line or bracket**, whether they have a rest or not.

Quaver, semiquaver or shorter triplets should be beamed together, have the number 3 and **no bracket or curved line.** If there is a rest is in the middle, then a beam should join the first and last notes.

But there is an exception! When they have a rest on the first or last place of the group. In that case, **a bracket or curved line should join the rest and the remaining two notes**.

| | With bracket | Without bracket |
| | | Beamed together |

With Rests

First place

In the middle

Last place

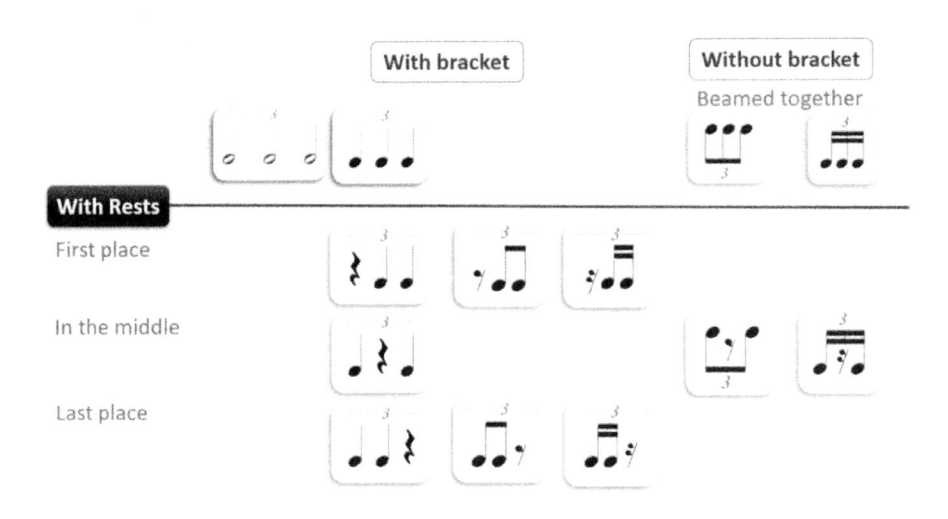

The 3s may be omitted in a passage of continuous triplets, once the pattern has been established, in ostinati or where the triplets are obvious.

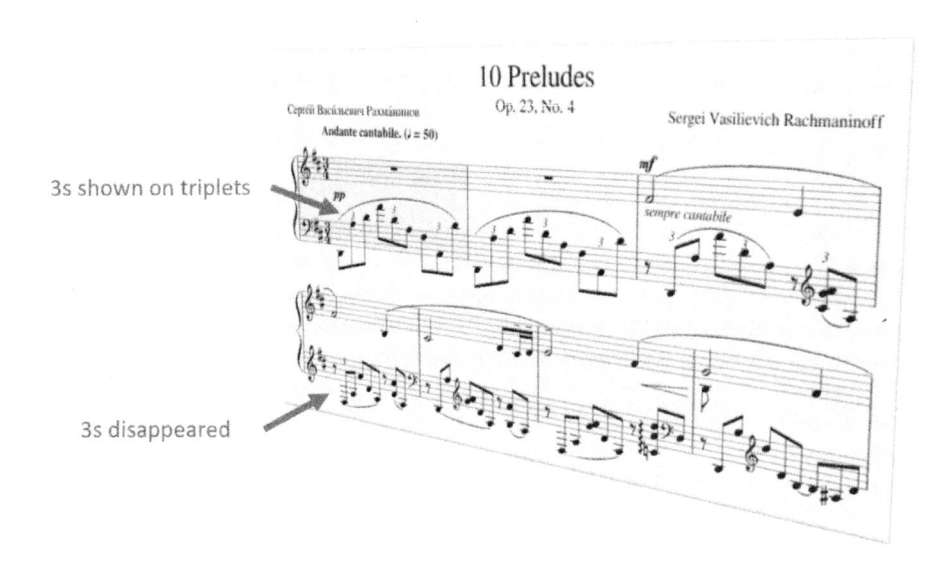

10 Preludes
Op. 23, No. 4
Sergei Vasilievich Rachmaninoff

3s shown on triplets

3s disappeared

Grouping Notes

In this chapter, you will learn how to group notes and rests together. It may look simple at this stage however, as you progress to higher levels, it will get more complicated, so it is important to build a strong foundation.

Beaming foundation

Notes with the same number of flags

Notes which have flags (for example, quavers or semiquavers) are normally grouped together under the same beam. This process is called beaming and it makes music easier to read.

If the notes to be beamed are quavers, one beam will join them all.

If they are semiquavers, a double beam is needed.

Notes with different number of flags

Notes of different durations can also be beamed together.

Dotted notes

Dotted notes can also be grouped under the same beam.

When a dotted note is beamed to a quicker note, the tail of the quick note should appear as a short beam pointing towards the dotted note.

Time signatures with a crotchet beat

Beaming Quavers

When two or more quavers are played in one crotchet beat or in two or more consecutive beats, they are usually beamed together.

Depending on the time signature, there are different rules to learn how to beam quavers properly.

In 2/4

In a 2/4 bar, a pair of quavers must be beamed together.

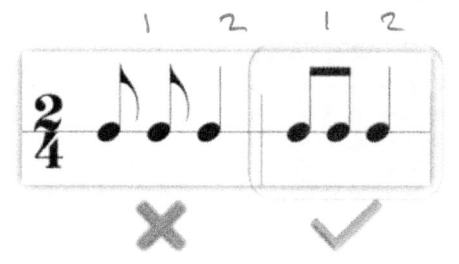

If there are four quavers in the bar, the four of them should be joined.

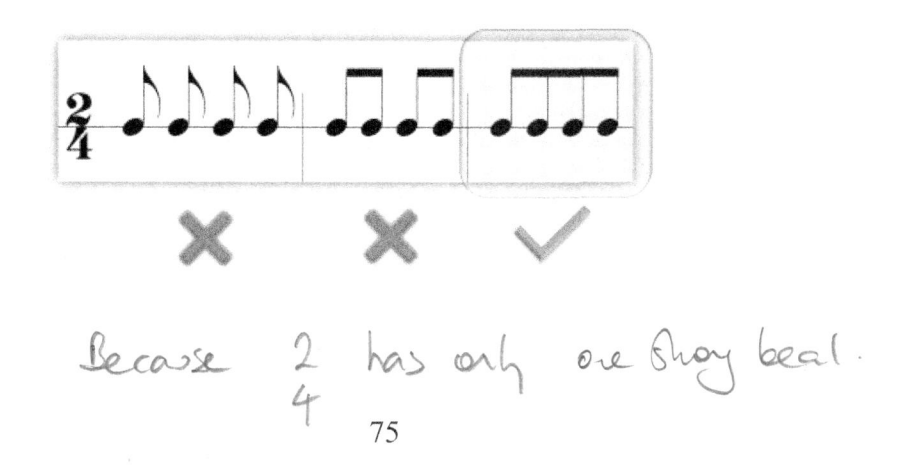

Because 2/4 has only one strong beat.

In 3/4

In a 3/4 time signature, any two, four or six consecutive quavers are beamed together:

Not always though!

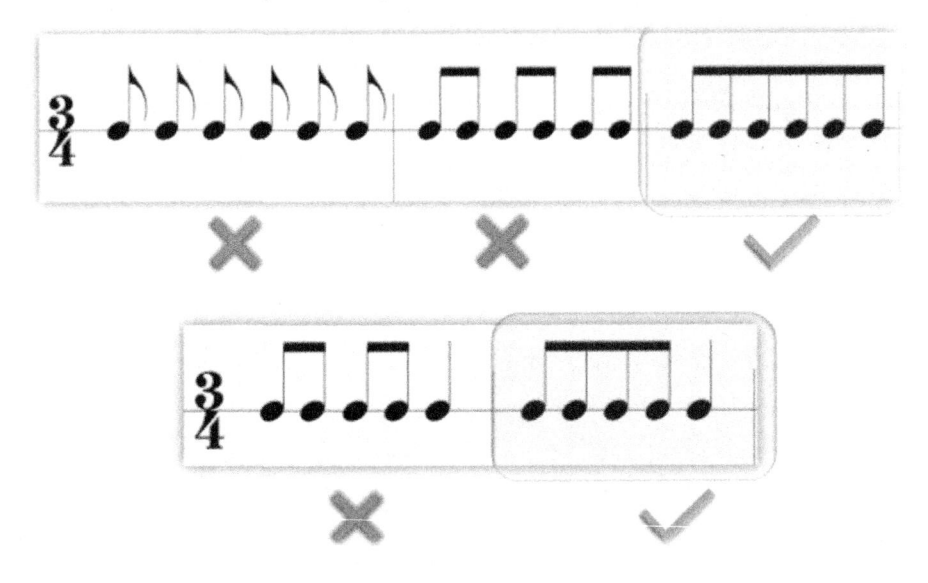

In 4/4

Beaming quavers in a 4/4 requires more attention than in other time signatures because the second beat can never be joined to the third.

The secret to get it right is to imagine a **hidden barrier** that separates beat 2 from 3. Never cross it with a beam!

To emphesise the beat. If you beam across there is no emphesis on strong beats + weak beats. Can't beam a weak beat to a strong beat.

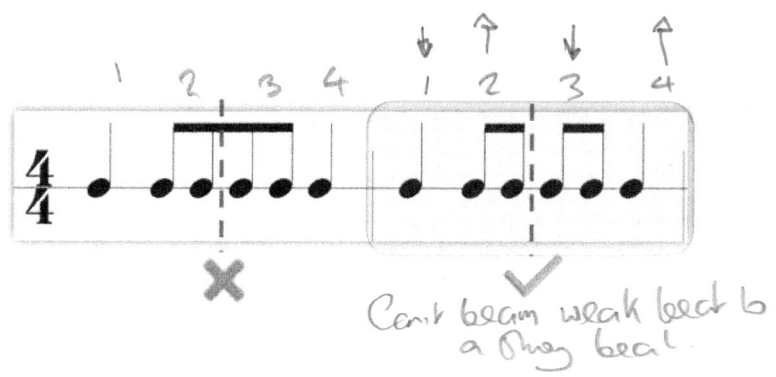

The good news is that there are no other problems between beat one and two or three to four.

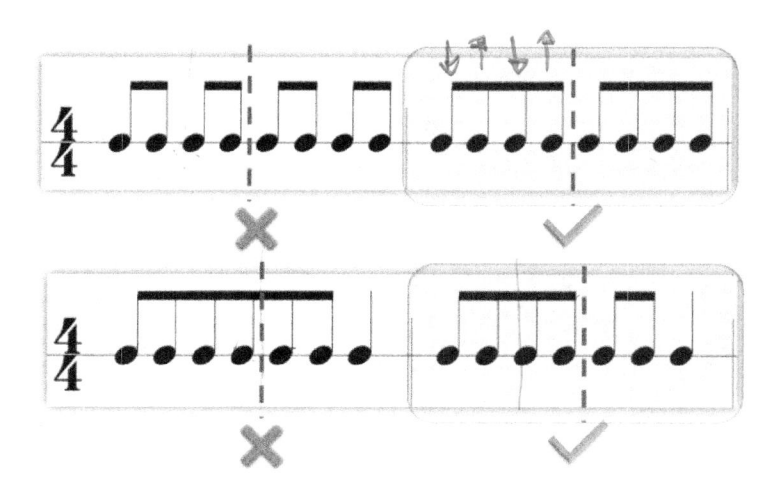

Beaming Semiquavers

To beam a group of semiquavers or a combination of quavers and semiquavers, you need to join the notes together for **a maximum of one beat**.

For example, beaming 8 semiquavers together in a 2/4 would not be correct because we would be joining two beats together. We need to separate them into two groups of four to respect the maximum allowed. When beaming semiquavers, you can also apply the tip of the hidden barrier between different beats.

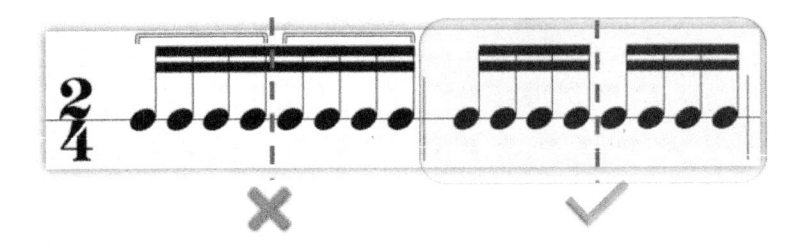

Let's look at other examples. If there is a combination of quavers and semiquavers, they should also be beamed together under the same single beat.

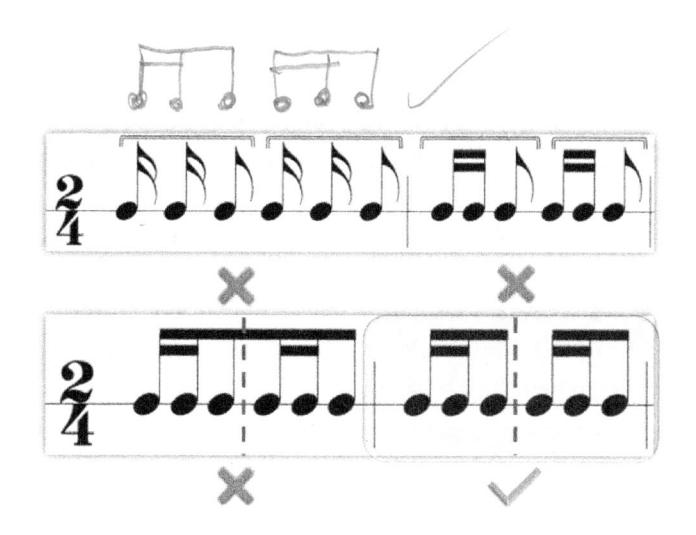

And here are some more examples in 3/4 and 4/4.

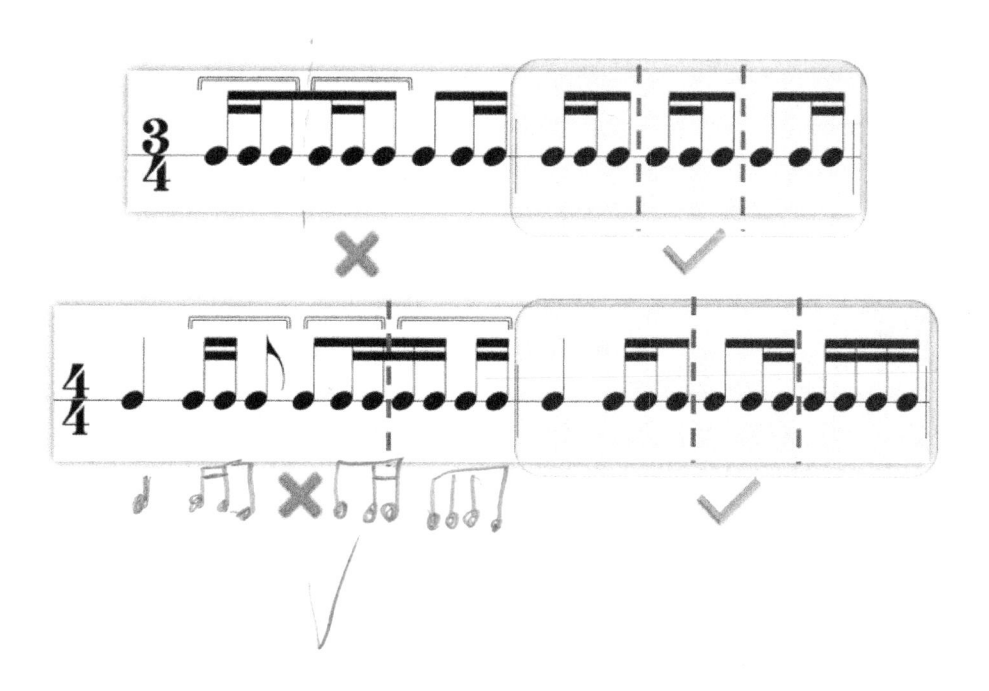

Beaming Dotted Rhythms

Dotted rhythms should also be joined in the same beat. For example, if I have a dotted quaver plus two semiquavers together plus another dotted quaver, it will not be correct because I would not be respecting the hidden barrier. If I separate the semiquavers now, I would separate the beats correctly, however, the dotted quaver must be beamed to the semiquaver.

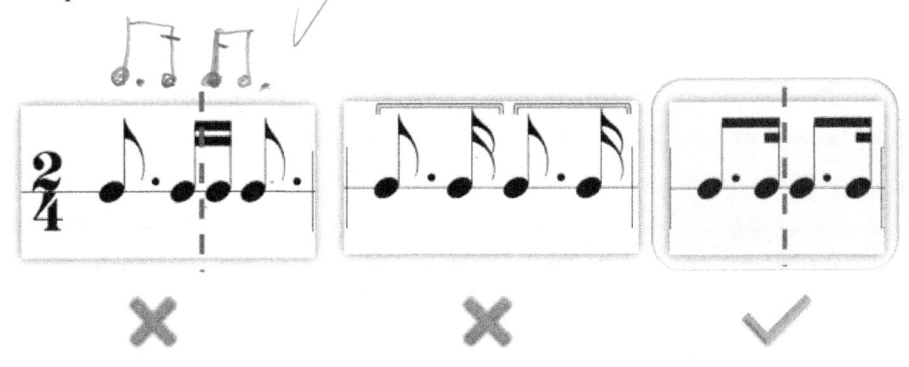

Avoid ties

You should also avoid ties as much as possible. Ties will become a bit confusing as you progress through the grades. But don't panic, in this level you only need to know these two rhythms:

In a 2/4, a dotted crotchet plus a quaver is better than a tie.

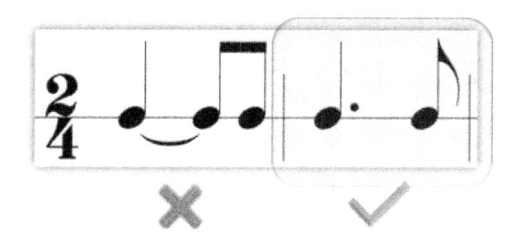

And in 4/4, a minim looks better than two tied crotchets because it makes a syncopated pattern. We will learn more about syncopation shortly.

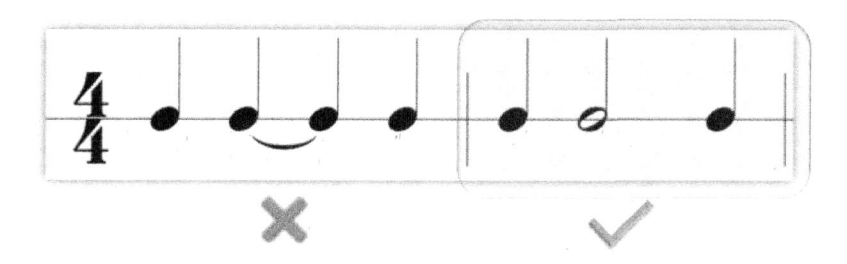

Syncopation

When the natural accentuation of a bar is moved, lengthening a note from a weak beat to a strong one, the rhythm created is called syncopation.

The two syncopated patterns that you need to recognise for Grade 2 are the ones in 2/4 and 4/4.

Syncopation can get very sophisticated but at the moment, you only need to remember that **these rhythms break the normal rules for grouping notes:**

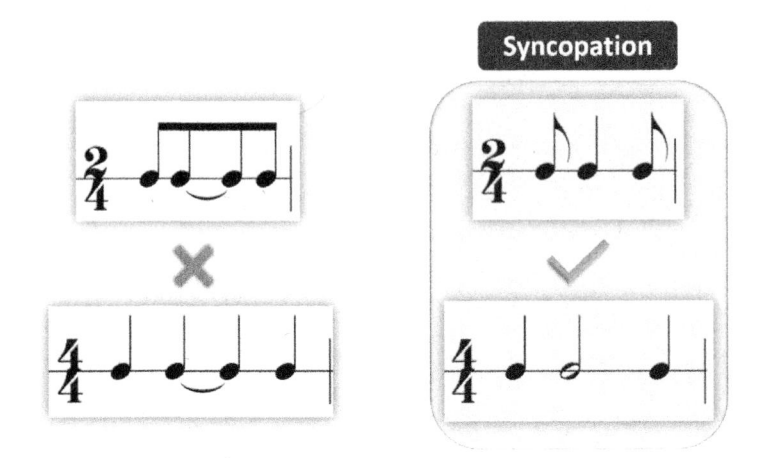

By the way! The notes are spaced out in such way as to show the length of the note values. This makes the music easy to sight read.

Rests in 2/4, 3/4, 4/4

Rests can also be grouped together to facilitate reading. The same way that there are rules to beam quavers, there are rules to group rests:

If two or more consecutive beats are left silent, we need to follow the following rules:

Grouping rests in 3/4: Use **two crotchet rests** where there are two consecutive beats of silence.

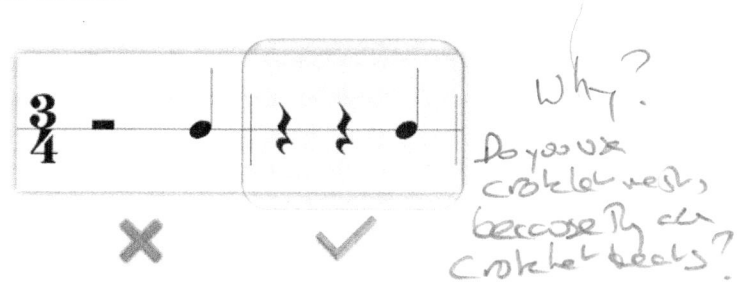

[Handwritten annotation: "Why? Do you use crotchet rests, because they are crotchet beats?"]

Grouping rests in 4/4: The hidden barrier rule applies to rests in 4/4. **A minim rest cannot be used to join the second to third beats.**

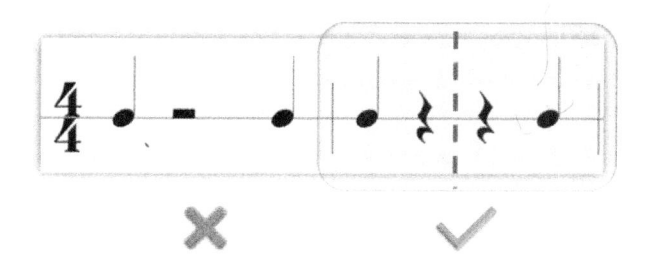

You should use a minim rest only where it would be possible to beam four quavers together. **If the silent beats are one to two or three to four, we must use the minim rests.**

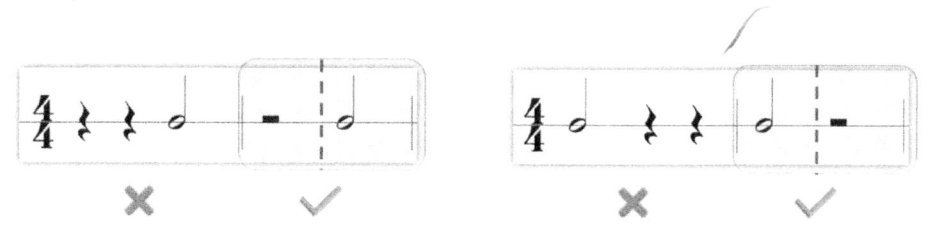

Time signatures with a minim beat

So far, we have only talked about grouping and beaming in time signatures with a crotchet as the beat. We will now continue learning how to group notes and rests in time signatures with a minim or a quaver as the beat.

Beaming quavers and semiquavers in 2/2, 3/2, 4/2

When **four quavers** are played in **one minim beat**, they should be **beamed together**.

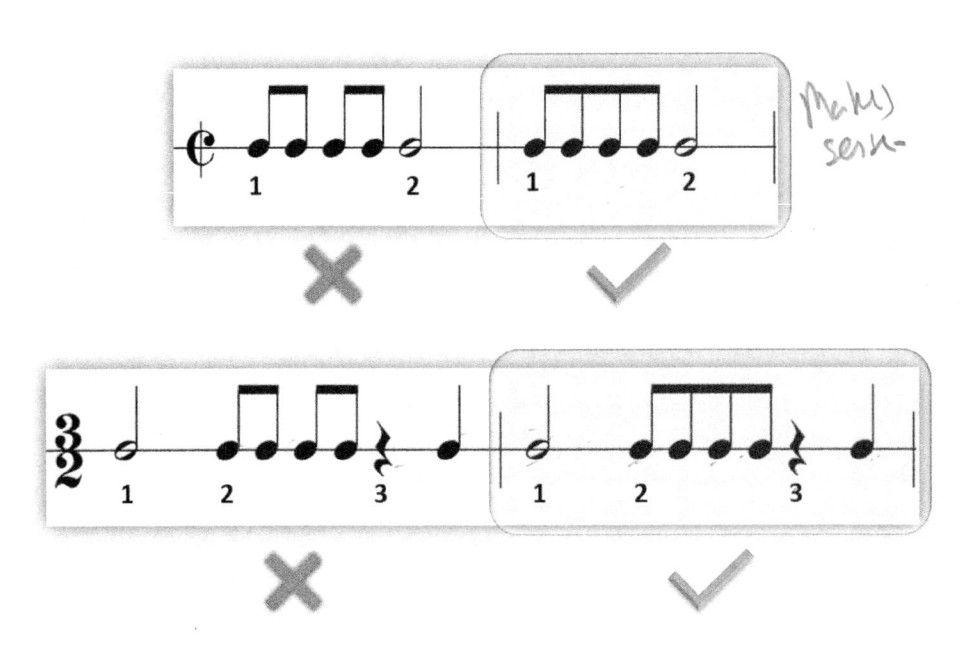

In the case of the **semiquavers, never beam more than four**. If there are eight consecutive semiquavers, then make **two groups of four**. In other words, beam together four semiquavers which could be replaced by a crotchet.

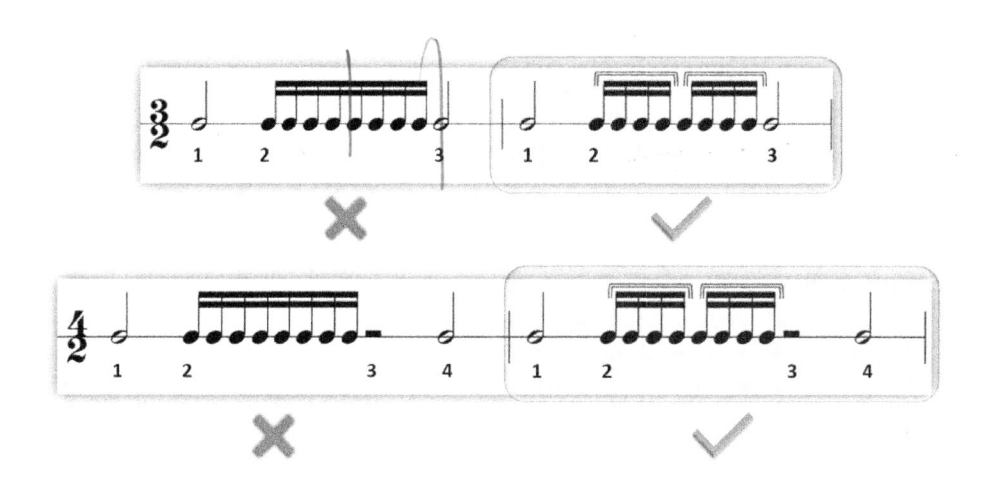

Rests in 2/2, 3/2, 4/2

If two or more consecutive beats are left silent, we need to follow the following rules:

Grouping rests in 2/2

The rule is **"a new beat needs a new rest"**. Look at some examples:

There are two minim beats per bar, and they should be clearly visible. **Never join the first beat with the second and never write more rests than needed**. In this example, the way of writing the rests is not correct because there are more than I need. I should group them as much as possible.

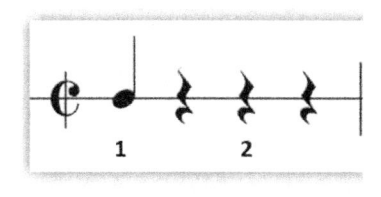

This other combination, will not be correct either because I am crossing beats with the dotted minim rest and not respecting the rule "a new beat needs a new rest". In the case of 2/2, the rule of the hidden barrier to separate the two beats can also be applied.

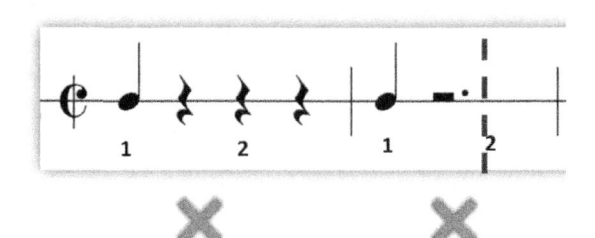

The correct way of grouping these rests would be:

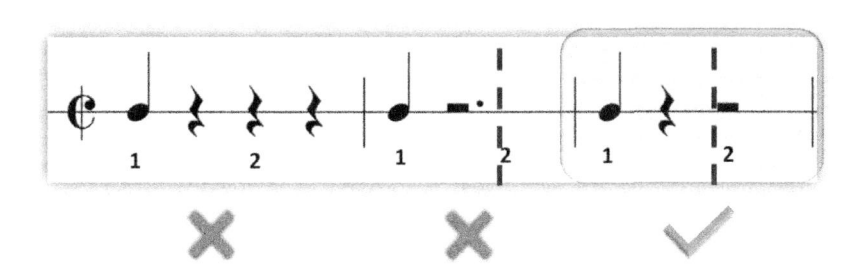

Here are some more examples:

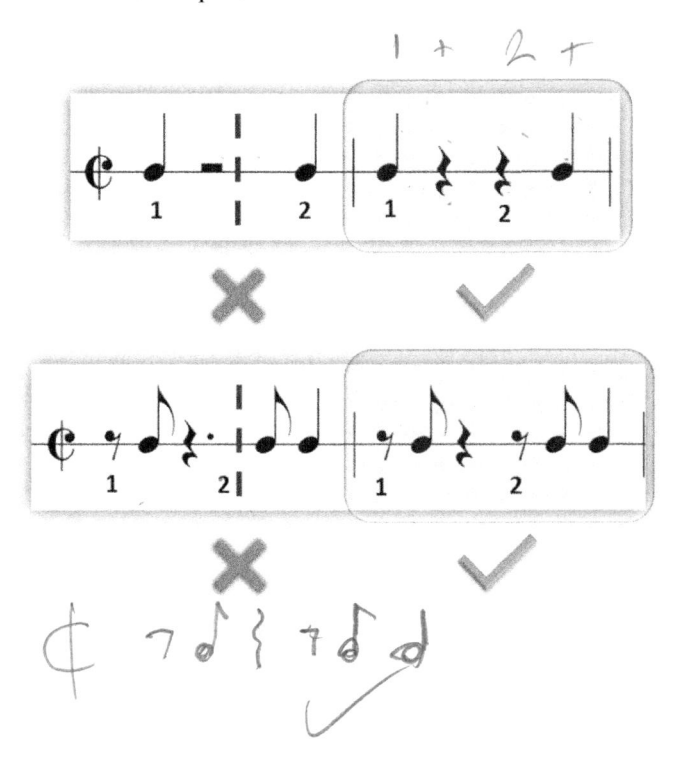

Grouping rests in 3/2

The rule still is **"a new beat needs a new rest"**. Look at some examples.

There are three minim beats per bar, and they should be clearly visible. **Never join one beat with the next and never write more rests than needed**. In this example, the way of writing the rests is not correct because there are more than I need. I should group them as much as possible.

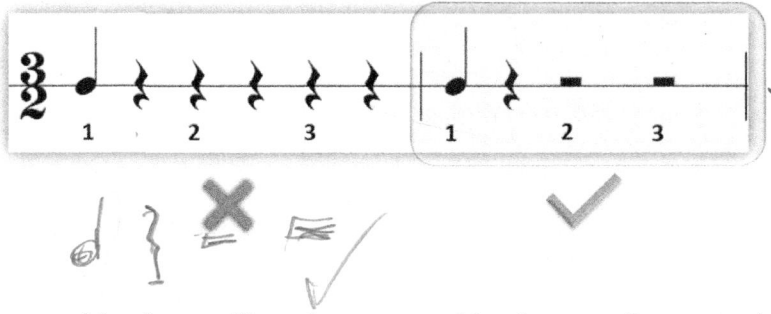

This other combination, will not be correct either because I am crossing beats with the minim rests and not respecting the rule "a new beat needs a new rest".

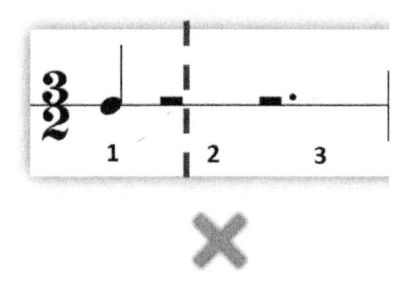

88

The correct way of grouping these rests would be:

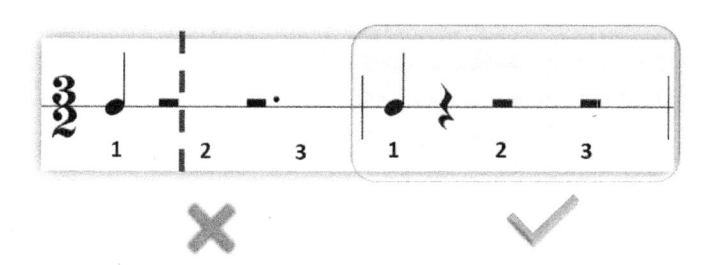

Here are some more examples:

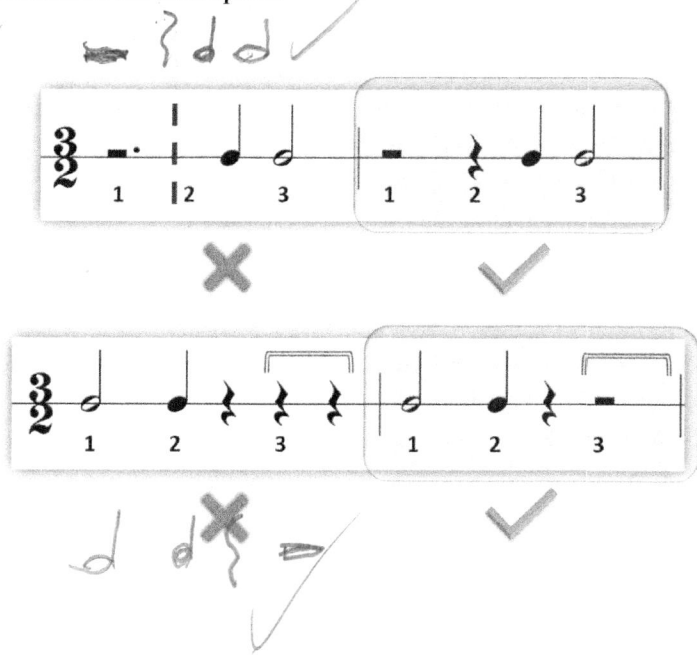

Grouping rests in 4/2

The hidden barrier rule applies to rests in 4/2. **A semibreve rest cannot be used to join the second to third beats.**

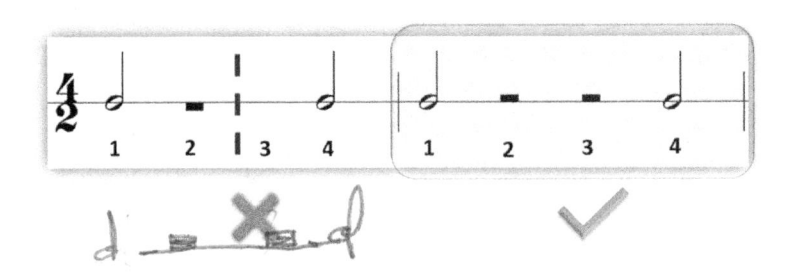

You should use a semibreve rest only if **the silent beats are one to two or three to four.**

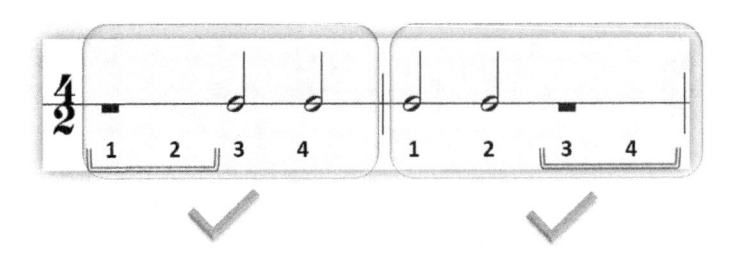

Avoid ties

You should keep avoiding ties as much as possible. Use a semibreve instead of two tied notes where possible.

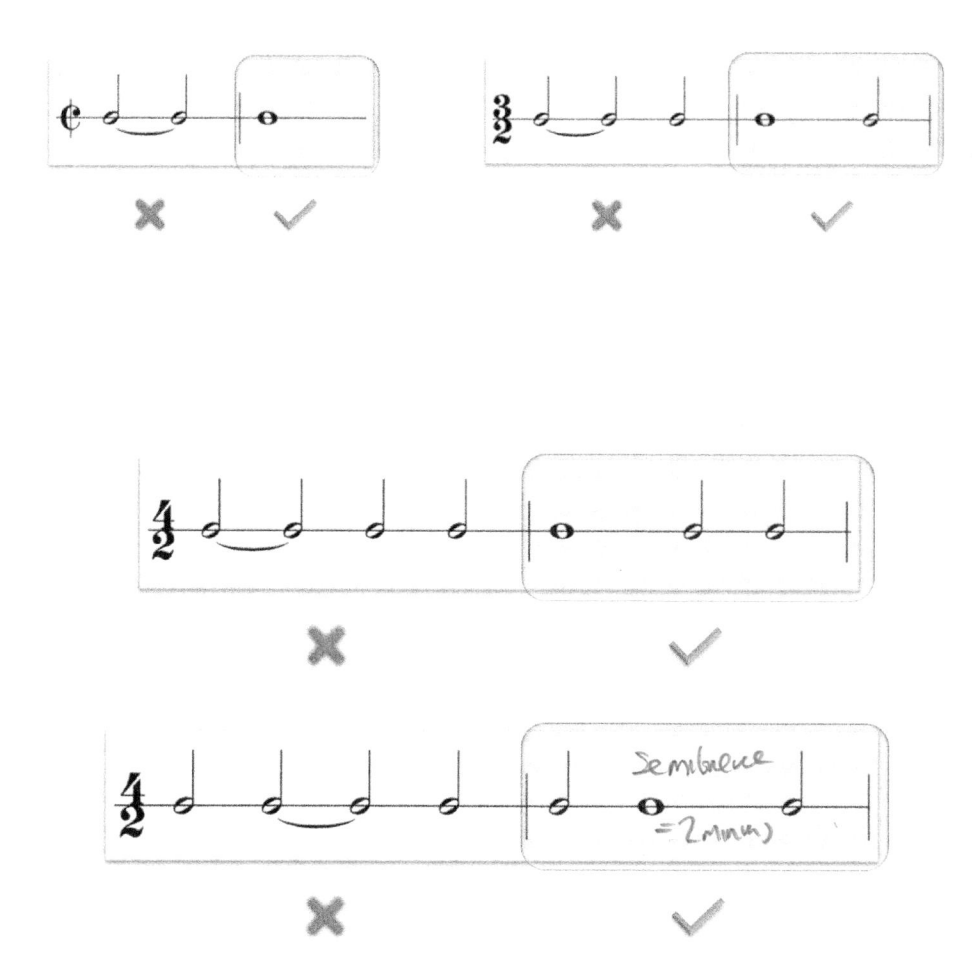

Watch out the stems!

When beaming together a group of high and low notes, **the direction of the stems should be the same for all**. How can we decide whether they point upwards or downwards?

Nothing to worry about. **The direction of the stems will be given by the furthest note from the middle line**. Here is an example:

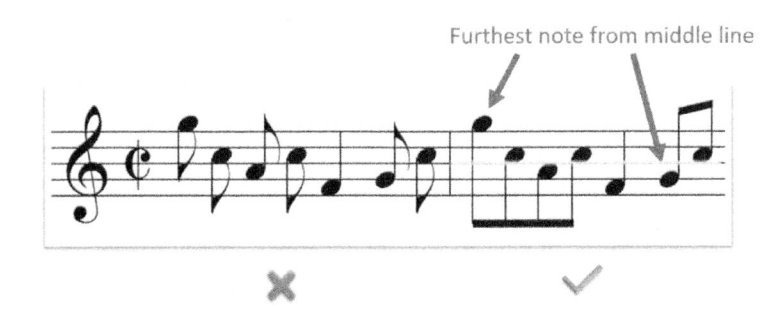

Time signatures with a quaver beat

Beaming quavers and semiquavers in 3/8

Easy. As this is a short bar, **beam together quavers or semiquavers that make a complete bar. 3/8 is the only time signature where more than four semiquavers should be beamed together.**

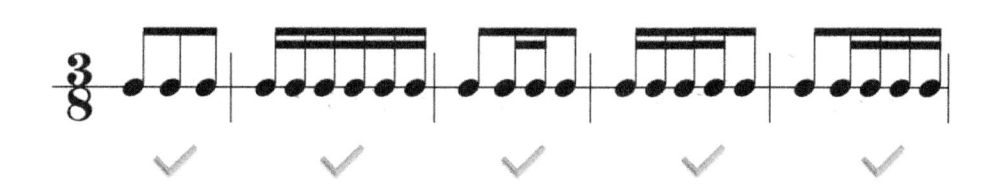

Rests in 3/8

If two or more consecutive beats are left silent, we need to follow the following rules:

The rule is **"a new beat needs a new rest"**. Look at some examples:

There are three quaver beats per bar, and they should be clearly visible. **Never join one beat with the next and never write more rests than needed.**

In this example, the way of writing the rests is not correct because there are more than I need. I should group them as much as possible.

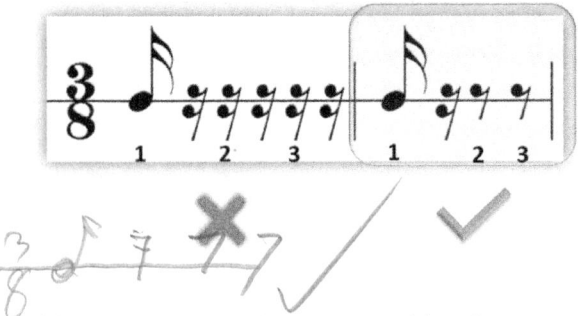

This other combination, will not be correct either because I am crossing beats with the quaver rests and not respecting the rule "a new beat needs a new rest". The correct way of grouping these rests would be:

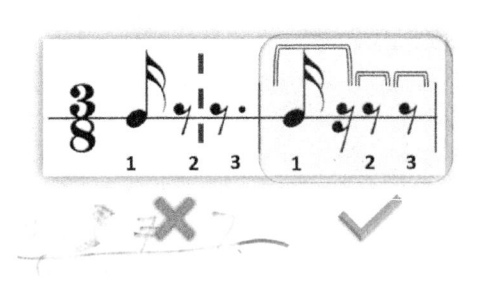

Here are some more examples:

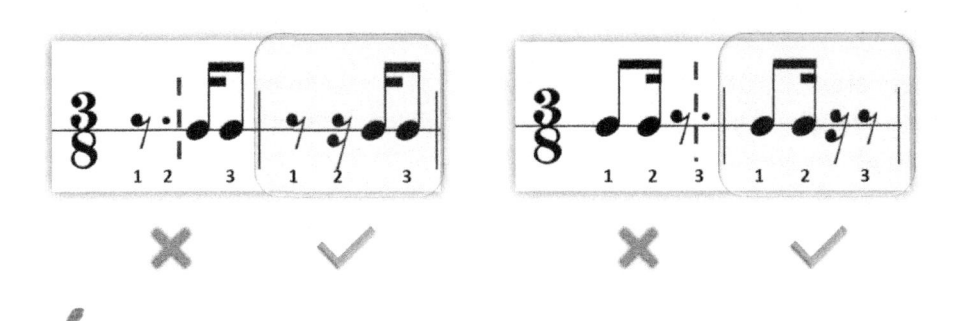

Grouping Rests – General rules
Whole Bar Rest

Last but not least, in case all beats were silent, we need to draw a **semibreve rest for any silent full bar**. In other words, a whole bar of silence should have a semibreve rest, **regardless of the time signature.**

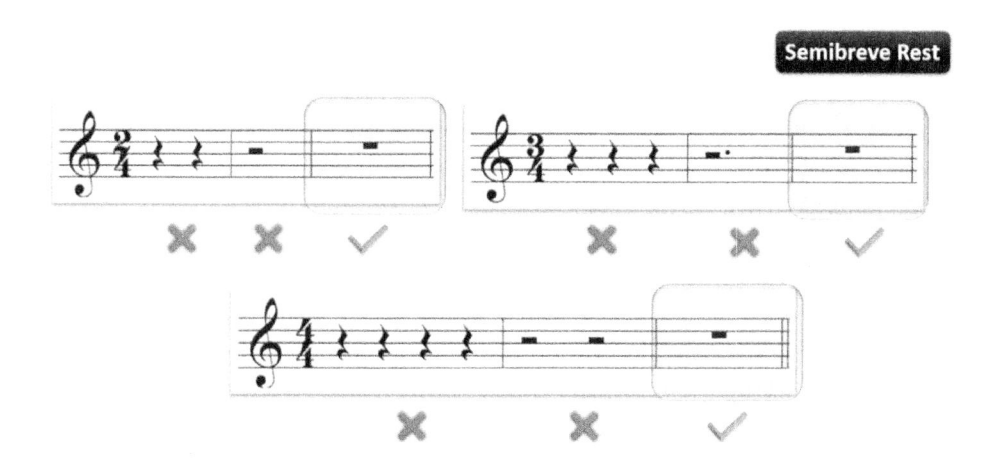

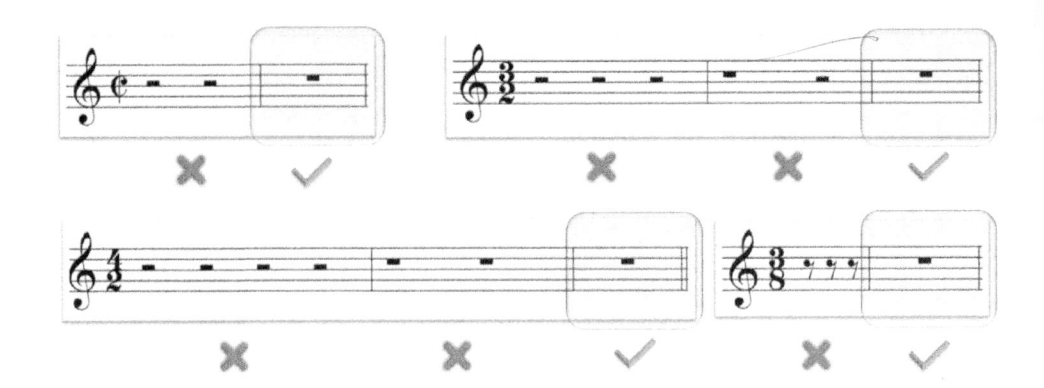

It is worth mentioning that even though these are the rules we must follow when beaming and grouping, composers sometimes break the rules to express phrasing or other performance related ideas.

Grouping rests shorter than a beat

Sometimes, you will need to group rests shorter than a beat. In these cases, group the notes and rests **to separate half-beats.**

For example, this quaver rest between the two semiquavers is not correct because the half beats are not easily visible. The correct notation in this case is two semiquaver rests.

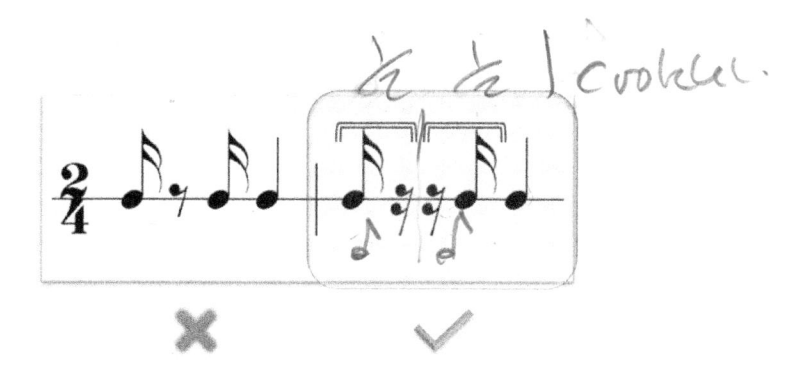

In the second example, the semiquaver rest should follow the semiquaver to represent half beat. Then the quaver rest will represent the other half.

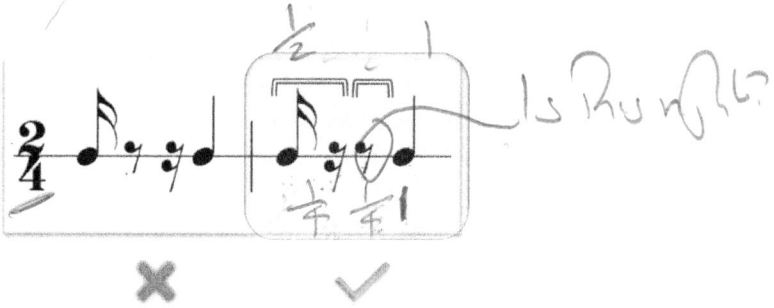

In this other example in 2/2, the quaver rest should follow the quaver as they will make together half beat. The crotchet rest afterwards will complete the other half.

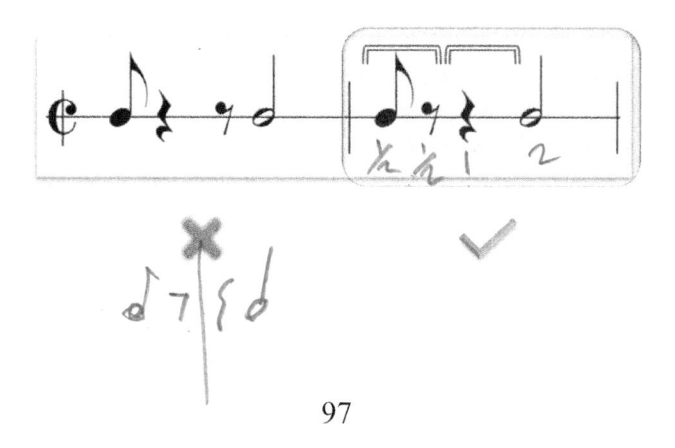

Accidentals

Accidentals are signs written on the left side of a note that represent an alteration on its pitch. This modification can raise or lower the sound.

- A flat lowers the pitch of a note by a semitone.
- A sharp raises the pitch of a note by a semitone.
- And the natural sign restores the original pitch of the note.

FLAT — Lowers a note

NATURAL — Restores original pitch

SHARP — Raises a note

After an accidental is written, it will continue to affect any following notes of the same pitch in the same bar. However, it will not affect notes of the same letter name in a different octave.

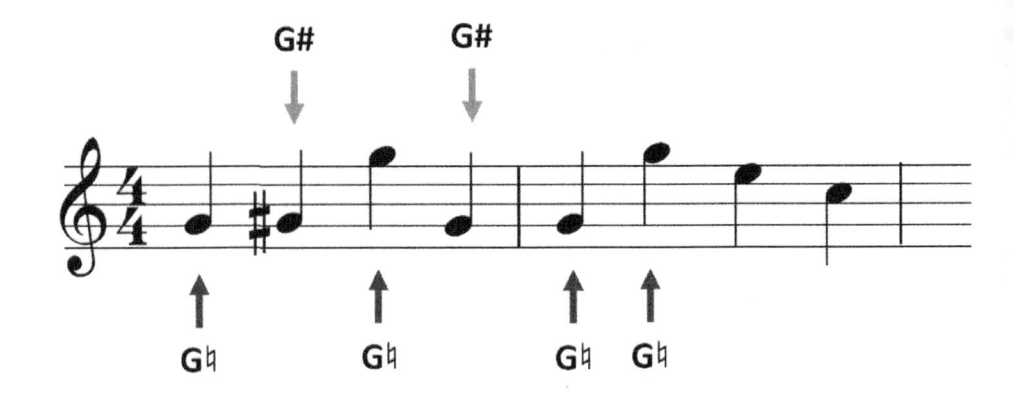

If both octaves are to be altered, another accidental should be added.

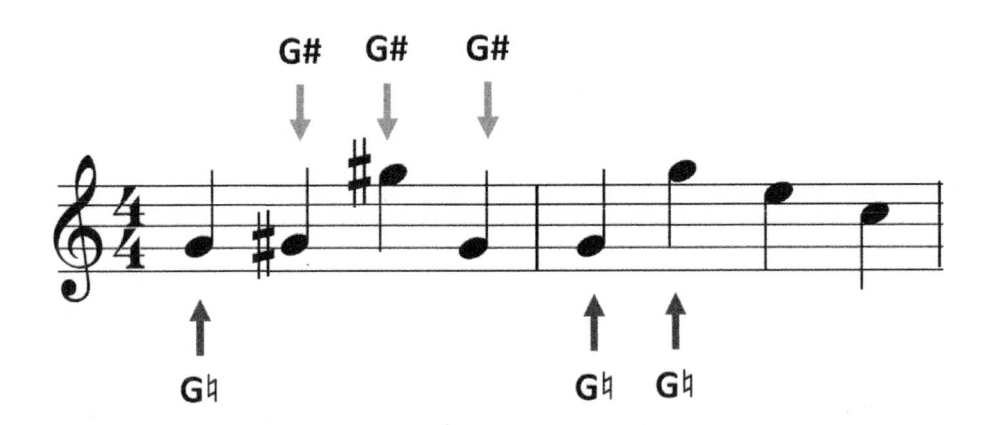

In addition to this, if an accidental is applied to tied notes, it will continue to affect the held note, even across bar lines.

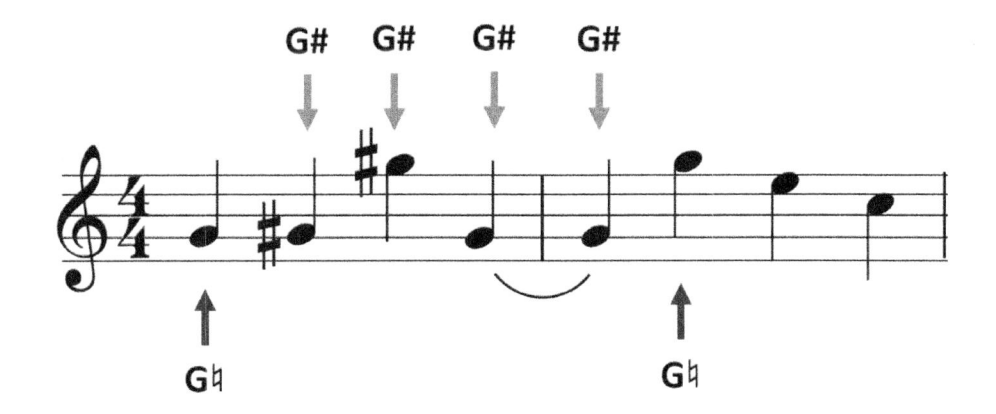

If an accidental appears only occasionally, it is unlikely to make any alteration to the key. However, if it is used more frequently, it could involve a change of key, although it may not be necessary to write a new key signature.

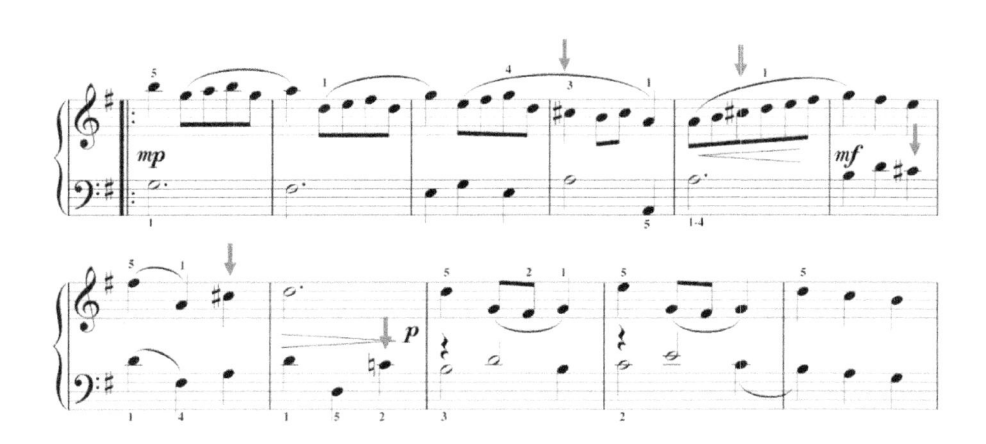

Writing an accidental

When writing an accidental we need to be very precise and draw the sign **on the same line or space that the note it relates to**.

We should also tilt the lines across the sharp sign so that it does not get muddled up with the stave lines and become difficult to read.

Also remember that they are always placed **on the left side of the note-head**.

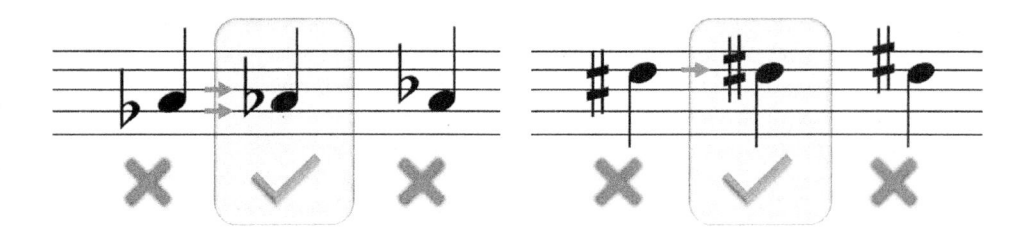

Cancelling an accidental

An accidental lasts **until the end of the bar**.

If we wanted to restore the original pitch on later notes within the same bar, we would need to use a natural sign.

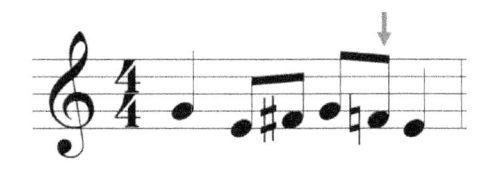

Natural signs are also used to cancel the effect of a sharp or flat in the key signature.

Keys and Key Signatures

The key of a piece is the tonality on which it is composed. We can think of the key as the mood, emotion or even colour that music can transmit.

It is easier to understand if we listen to how the key can affect music and how different *Twinkle Twinkle Little Star sounds* if it is played in a different key. Try playing this excerpt at home:

The sharps or flats placed immediately after the clef and before the time signature are called key signature and represent the key of the piece.

Major and minor modes

In Grade 1, you learned some major keys and major scales, as well as their key signatures. In Grade 2, you will also work on the minor mode.

First of all, we need to clarify. What is a mode? A mode is basically the type of scale used in a piece of music.

As we listened before with the example of Twinkle Twinkle played in C Major and then in C Minor, the mode puts certain **character** to the music.

Musical modes originated in ancient Greece long before people started thinking about pieces of music having keys.

There are many musical modes: Ionian, Dorian, Phrygian, Lydian, Mixolydian, Aeolian and Locrian. Luckily, you only need to know major and minor modes.

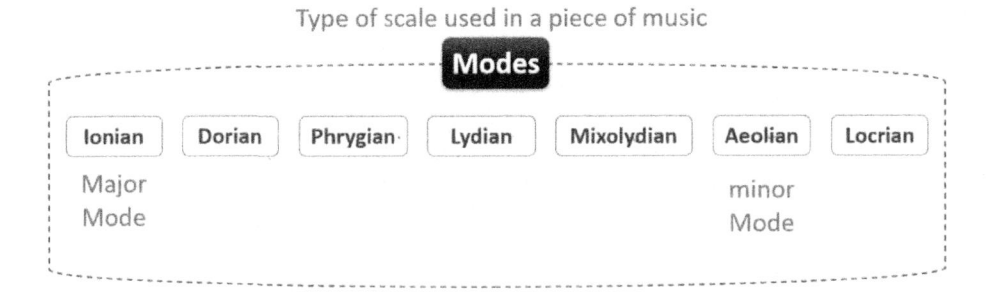

Type of scale used in a piece of music

Modes

| Ionian | Dorian | Phrygian | Lydian | Mixolydian | Aeolian | Locrian |

Major Mode   minor Mode

In the previous level, you learned the Major keys of some key signatures. At this stage, you should also know that major and minor keys which share the same key signature are said to be "relatives" of each other.

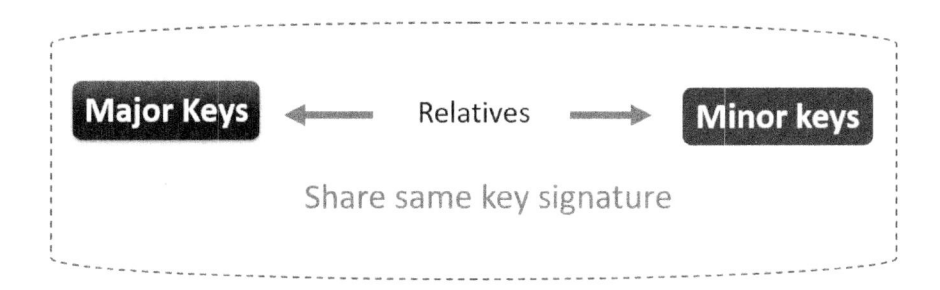

Major Keys ← Relatives → **Minor keys**

Share same key signature

All Major keys have a relative minor key, just like a little brother. The same way that siblings share the same parents, **relative major and minor keys share the same key signature**.

In Grade 2, you will work on A minor, E minor and D minor.

A minor — C MAJ

E minor — G MAJ

D minor — F MAJ

But, how do I know what is the relative minor of a major scale and viceversa? **Minor scales start a tone and a half (minor 3rd) below their relative major scale.**

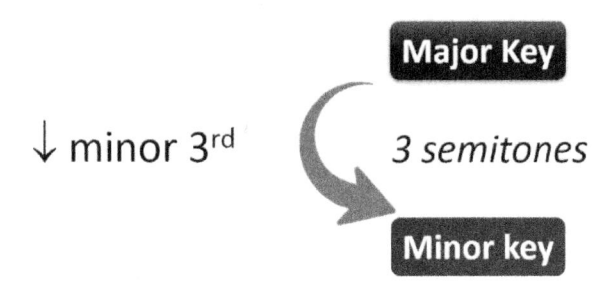

↓ minor 3rd

Major Key

3 semitones

Minor key

For example, if I want to find the relative minor of C Major, I need to count a tone and half down from C. I will get to A so A minor will be the relative minor of C Major.

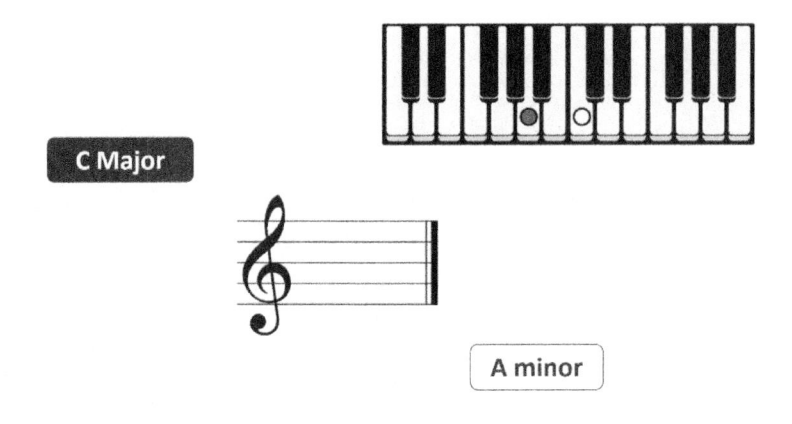

C Major

A minor

If I want to do the opposite and find the relative major of a minor key, then the tone and a half should be ascending.

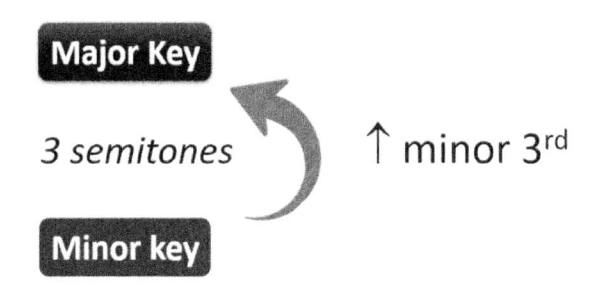

Major Key

3 semitones ↑ minor 3rd

Minor key

For example, if we want to find the relative major of E minor, we will get to G so G Major will be the relative major of E minor.

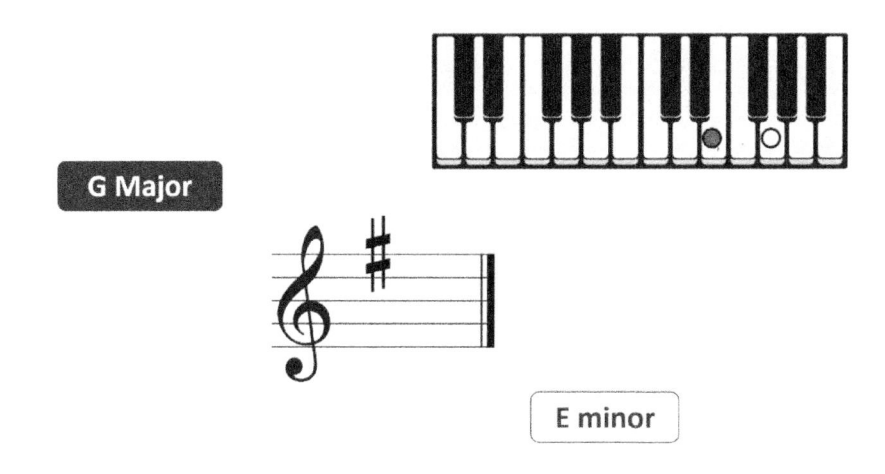

G Major

E minor

Practice finding as many major and minor relatives as possible, as this will be very helpful when key signatures get more complicated in the future.

Grade 2 Key Signatures

The keys of G Major and E Minor, have 1 sharp in the key signature (F#)

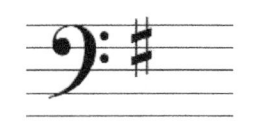

The keys of D Major and B Minor, have 2 sharps in the key signature (F# and C#)

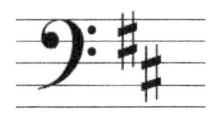

The keys of A Major and F# Minor, have 3 sharps in the key signature (F#, C# and G#)

The keys of F Major and D Minor, have 1 flat in the key signature (Bb)

The keys of Bb Major and G Minor, have 2 flats in the key signature (Bb, Eb)

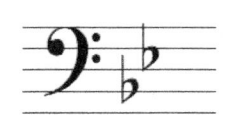

The keys of Eb Major and C minor, have 3 flats in the key signature (Bb, Eb, Ab)

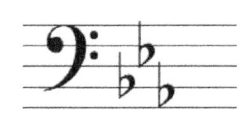

By the way! The keys of C Major and A minor have no sharps or flats in their key signature!

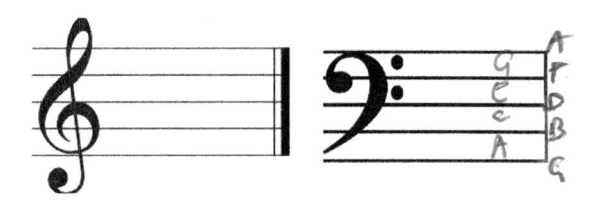

As you might have noticed, every time a new sharp or flat is added, the previous ones stay, and stay in the same place and order. The order of the flats and sharps is always the same and **must not be ignored**. If you read them aloud, you should also say them in the correct order.

- The order of the sharps is: F-C-G-D-A-E-B.
- And the order of the flats is the same sequence but backwards: B-E-A-D-G-C-F.

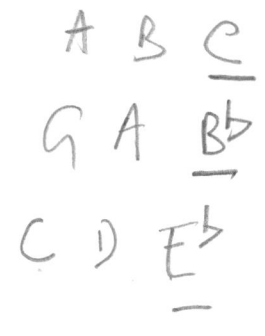

A B C
G A B♭
C D E♭

FCGDAEB   BEADGCF

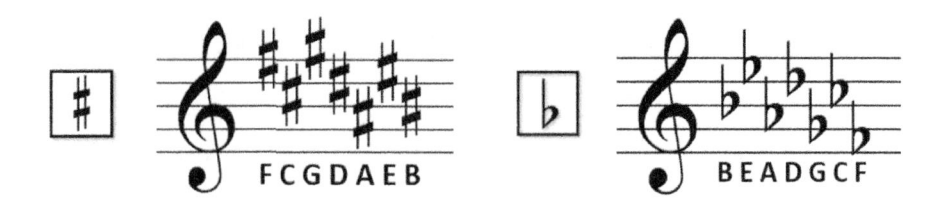

Learning this order by heart will help you not only with your theory exercises but also with your instrument's scales. It is also very important to remember to get ready for more advanced keys and their key signatures.

The sharps and flats in key signatures are not accidentals and affect to all the notes with the same letter name in the music, regardless of the octave or clef they are written in.

Writing Key Signatures

All sharps or flats in a key signature have a **specific place** were to be drawn.

For example, F sharp must be on the fifth line and never in the first space. In bass clef, B flat should be drawn on the second line and never above the stave. As you learn other key signatures, you will also need to learn how to draw them.

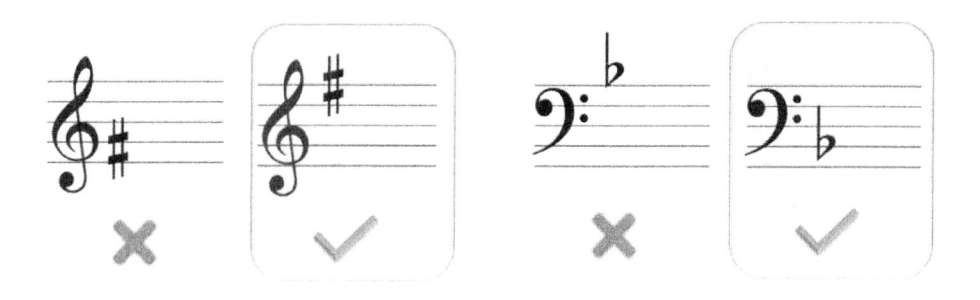

Last but not least, remember that key signatures, as well as clefs, must be written on every stave of a piece.

'Raindrop' Prelude op. 28 no. 15 - F. Chopin

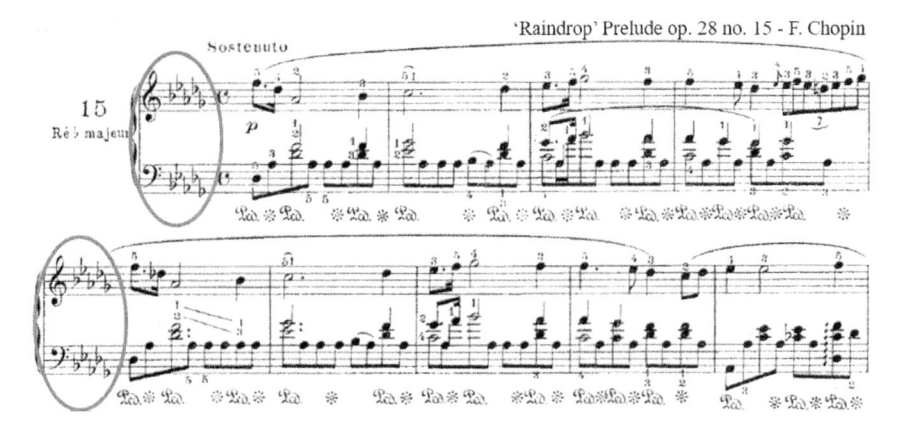

And also note that if the key has to be changed during the course of a piece, a double bar-line followed by the new key signature is needed:

The Circle of Fifths

The circle of fifths is a map of the keys used in music. As all maps, it shows you the way from one place to another. The circle of fifths will help you get from one key to another.

Let's learn how it works:

First, divide a circle into 12, just like a clock.

We will start from C Major and its relative A minor, because they are the keys with no sharps or flats in the key signature.

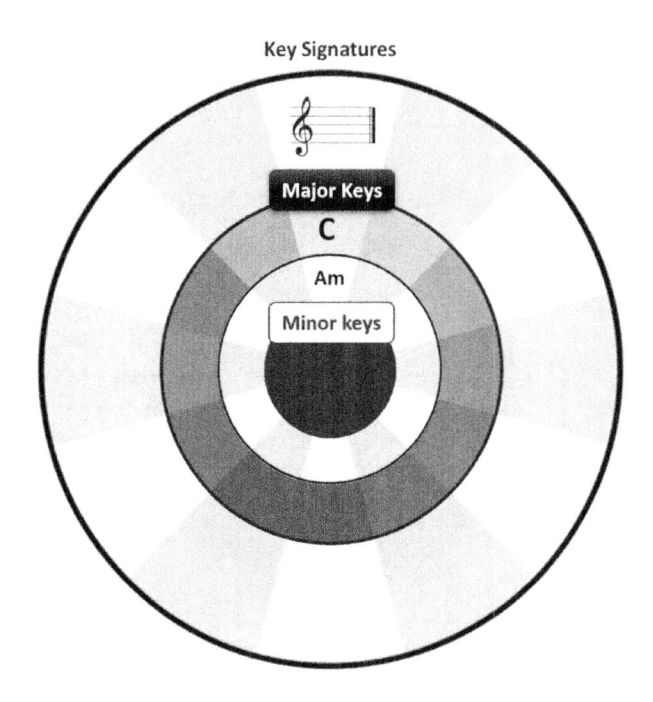

115

If we move clockwise around the circle, there will be sharps in the key signatures. If we move anticlockwise, there will be flats.

The order of the sharps or flats is always a fifth apart. This order is always the same and must not be ignored. If you read it aloud, you should also say them in the correct order:

F C G D A E B

The order of the flats is the same pattern but backwards:

B E A D G C F

When we say that a key has, for example, three sharps in the key signature, they will always be F, C, G. Or if it has four flats, they will be B, E, A, D and never any other or in a different order. Note that all key signatures have either sharps or flats, **never a mixture of both**.

The place where the sharps and flats are written in the stave, whether line or space, must also be the same. Changing a sign to a different octave would not be correct. (Visit the Key Signatures Chapter for more information).

Learning this order by heart will help you not only with your theory exercises but also with your instrument's scales.

As we move **clockwise** round the circle, each step (each key) will be a perfect **ascending** fifth from the last one. However, if we move **anticlockwise,** the interval from step to step is a perfect **descending** fifth, so we need to count down.

To find the next key after C Major, we need to count a perfect ascending fifth from C. It will be G, so the next key signature is G Major. The relative minor is E minor. The same process applies from step to step in this direction, so the following keys after G Major are D Major and B Minor, and the next ones are A Major and F# Minor.

If we move anticlockwise, the perfect fifth should be descending, so we would be counting down. Coming from C Major, we will find F Major, Bb Major and Eb Major and their relatives D minor, G minor and C minor.

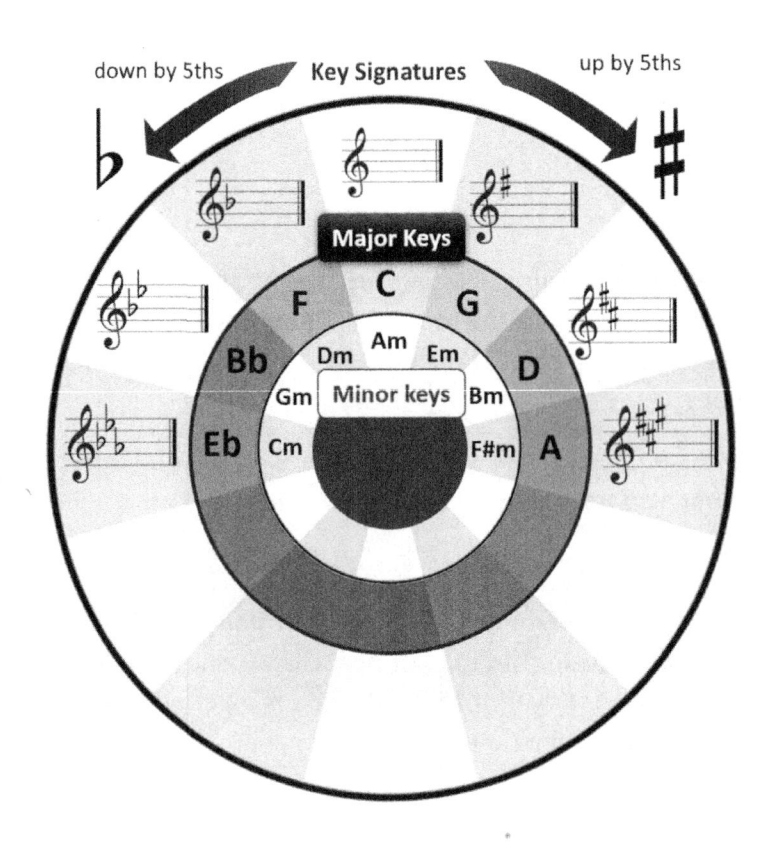

We could carry on working out the rest of the keys in the circle but in Grade 2, you only need to know these. The Circle of Fifths is a fascinating tool where music harmony settles its basis. If you learn it properly now, you will never forget it and it will accompany you for the rest of your music studies.

For a deeper explanation of the Circle of Fifths, please check this video out in our YouTube channel!

> ▶ **9 Secrets about the Circle of Fifths**
> https://youtu.be/oK_K6Ddlqt0

How to find the Major key of a Key Signature

For sharps, the last sharp in the key signature will be the seventh note of the major key. For example, if there are three sharps, the last one is G sharp. If G sharp is the seventh note, then the key signature is A Major.

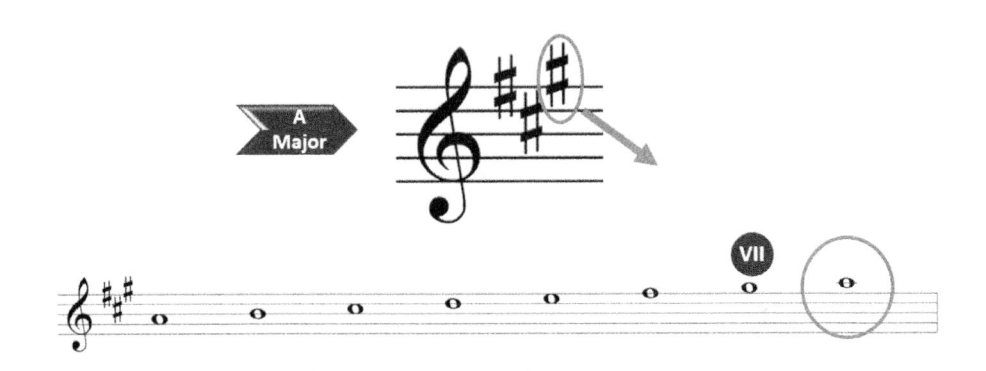

When there are two sharps and C# is the last sharp and the seventh note, we are in D Major.

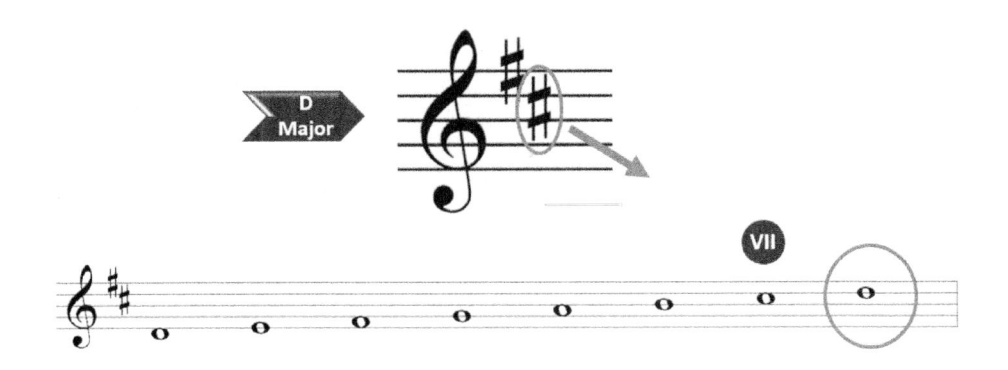

If there is only one sharp, it will be considered the last. So, if F sharp is the seventh note, then the key signature is G Major.

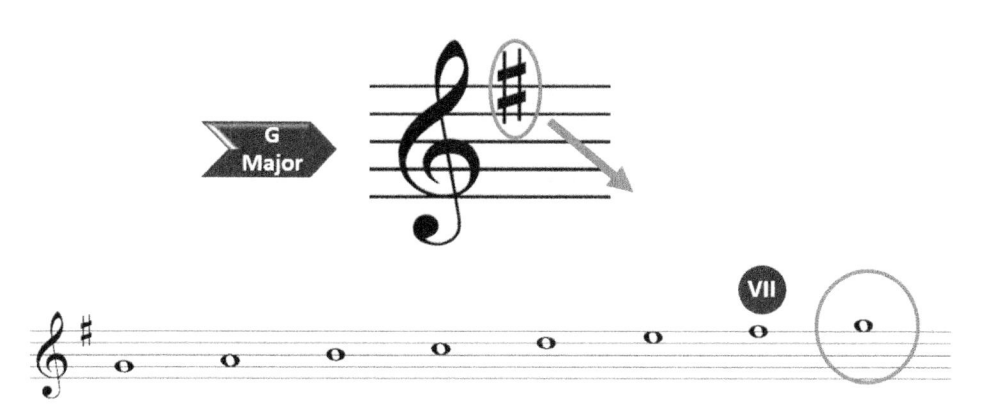

Flats work differently, as we need to look at the second last flat. That will give us the name of the major key.

But what happens if there is only one flat, how can I look at the second last if there isn't any? You need to remember the order of flats: B-E-A-D-G-C-F.

The previous of B will be the last of the sequence: F. Then the major key with one flat only will be F Major.

Flats order: B E A D G C F

How to find the key signature of a minor key

If you are looking for the key signature of a minor key, you need to find it **from the relative major key.** This means that, if you want to find out what is the key signature of G minor, you need to find the relative major first and then, its key signature.

Let's look at it in 3 easy steps:

1. From the key of G minor, **move a tone and a half up**.
2. You will get to Bb, so Bb Major is the relative major of G minor.
3. Now remember the circle of fifths and the order of the flats. **The second last flat is always the one that names the major key.**

G minor has therefore, two flats in its key signature.

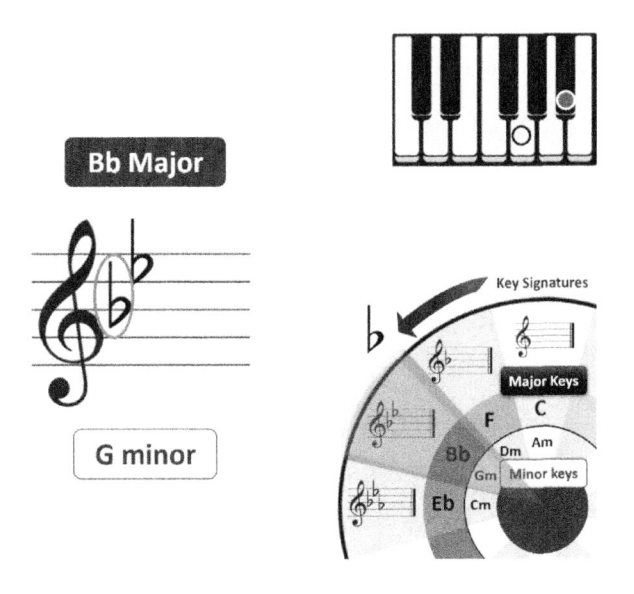

The most important concept to remember here is to find the key signature **from the relative major key**. Two **frequent mistakes** are:

➤ Considering the minor key as the second last flat. Going back to the previous example, a wrong answer would have been that G minor has 6 flats. The key which has 6 flats in its key signature is Gb Major. Pretty far from the right answer.

G minor

➤ Looking for the seventh note of the scale and considering that as the last sharp. **This trick does not work with minor scales!** Taking the example of G minor again, another incorrect answer would have been that G minor has 1 sharp. The key which has 1 sharp in the key signature is G Major. Again, not the right answer.

G minor

We will try another example, with sharps in this case.

What is the key signature of B minor?

1. From the key of B minor, **move a tone and a half up**.
2. You will get to D, so D Major is the relative major of B minor.
3. Now remember the circle of fifths and the order of the sharps. **The last sharp is always the seventh note of the major scale**. The seventh note of D Major is C#, so then C# would be the last sharp in my key signature.

B minor has therefore, two sharps in its key signature.

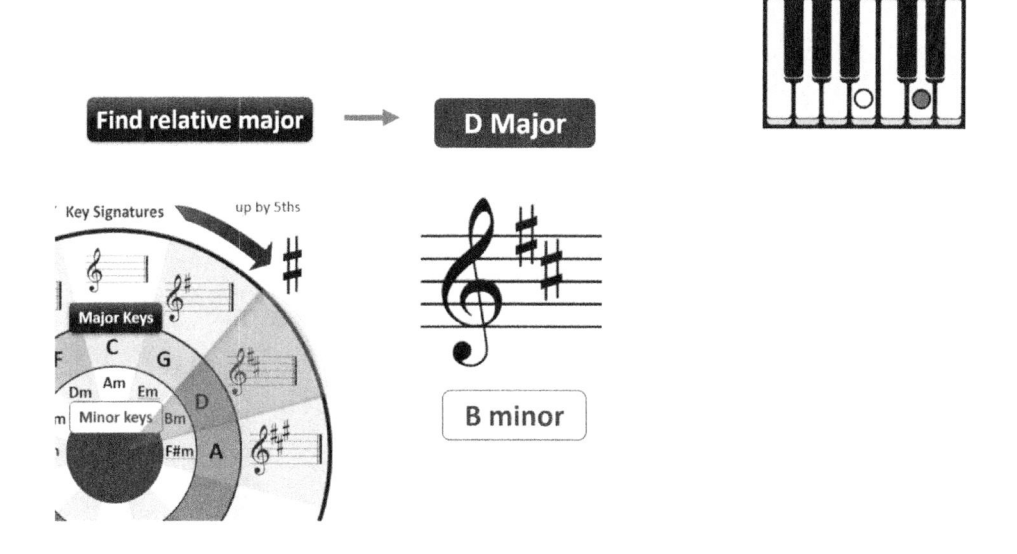

How to find the key of a piece

The key of a piece can be found by looking at its **key signature** and by checking any **accidental** it may have throughout. As relative keys share the same key signature, we may not be sure in some cases, but there are some questions that will help us find out.

Look at this example:

Ask yourself the following questions:
1. What is the key signature? *One sharp.*
2. Where is one sharp in the circle of fifths? *In the first step on the right side, so the key could be G Major or E minor.*
3. Is there any accidental in the music that could appear on any of the minor scales? *No. We may then discard E minor but we still need to continue checking to confirm G Major.*
4. What are the first and last notes? *G.*
5. Which tonic triad do they belong to? *G Major.*
6. Is there any place where the tonic triad may be spotted? *Yes, the first 2 bars are based around the tonic triad broken chord.*

We now have enough reasons to confirm this excerpt is in G Major.

Let's try another excerpt:

1. What is the key signature? *One flat.*
2. Where is one flat in the circle of fifths? *In the first step on the left side, so the key could be F Major or D minor.*
3. Is there any accidental in the music that could appear on any of the minor scales? *Yes, C# comes from the D minor harmonic scale. We may then discard F Major but we still need to continue checking to confirm D minor.*
4. What are the first and last notes? *A and D.*
5. Which tonic triad do they belong to? *D minor.*
6. Is there any place where the tonic triad may be spotted? *Yes, the first 3 bars are based around the tonic triad chord.*

We now have enough reasons to confirm this excerpt is in D minor.

Scales

Before scales are introduced, you should learn what tones and semitones are.

Tones and Semitones

In Western music, a **semitone is the smallest distance between two notes, and a tone is the sum of two semitones**.

Tones and semitones can also be described as steps or half steps. A half step is the distance between a note and the very next note, whether it is higher or lower. A whole step would be made of two half steps.

For example, there is a semitone between E and F or B and C, and also from F to F sharp.

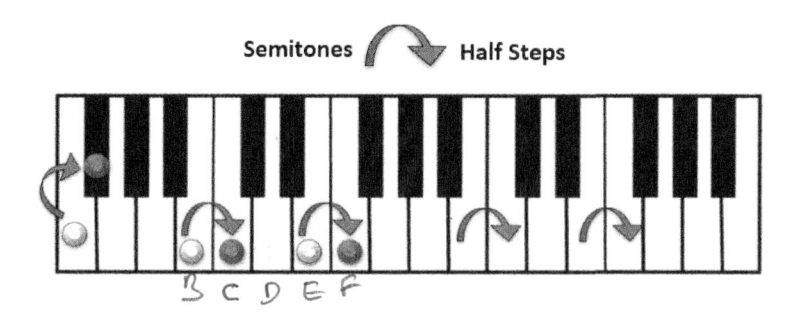

There are tones from E to F sharp, B to C sharp and C to D.

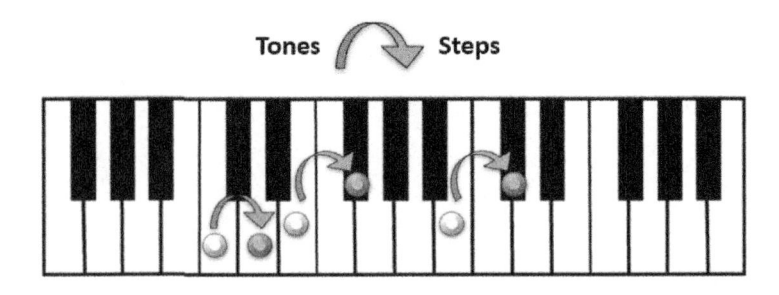

If you are still unsure, ask yourself this question: Can I fit a note between these two? If the answer is yes, then the distance is a tone. If the answer is no, then it will be a semitone.

Major Scales

A scale is a sequence of notes that follows a patterned order of tones and semitones. There are many types of scales and each of them will have a specific pattern.

All major scales follow the pattern of:

Tone – tone – semitone – Tone – tone – tone – semitone

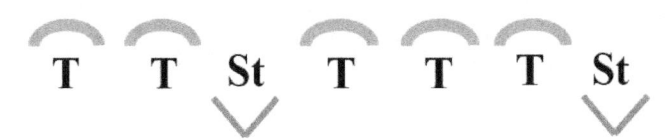

T   T   St   T   T   T   St

Grade 2 Major scales

C Major

Let's start with C Major:

From C to D there is a tone. From D to E there is a tone. From E to F there is a semitone.

From F to G there is a tone. From G to A there is a tone. From A to B there is a tone and from B to C there is a semitone.

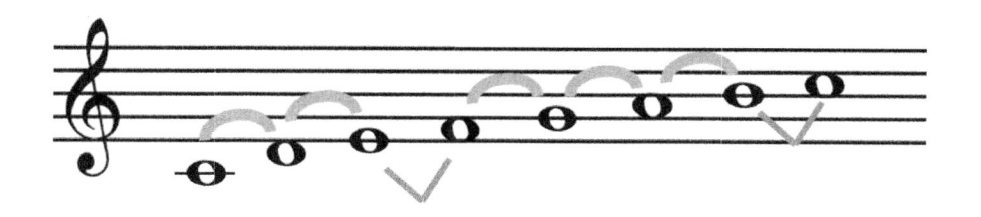

G Major

To make any other major scale, we need to apply the same pattern of tones and semitones and use sharps or flats if the distance needs to be adjusted.

The scale of G Major:

From G to A there is a tone. From A to B there is a tone. From B to C there is a semitone.

From C to D there is a tone. From D to E there is a tone.

So far so good as it does follow the Major scales pattern of tone-tone-semitone- tone-tone. However, there is now a semitone from E to F where there should be a tone. In order to follow the correct pattern, we have to alter the F and make it sharp. The distance will then be a tone from E to F sharp and also a semitone from F sharp to G.

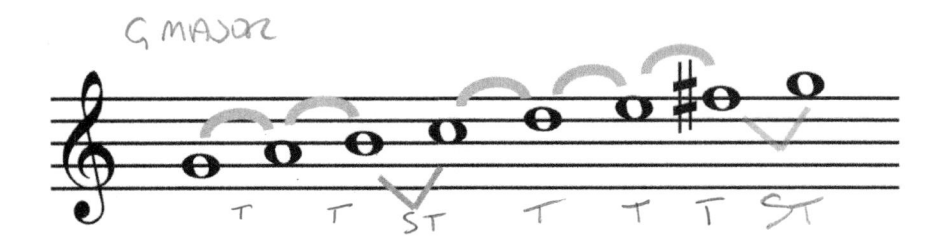

G MAJOR

D Major

More sharps and flats will be needed to adjust the distances in other scales.

From D to E there is a tone.

From E to F there is a semitone, but we need a tone, so we need to add a sharp to the F, which also makes a semitone to G.

From G to A there is a tone. From A to B there is a tone

But from B to C there is a semitone and we need a tone, so the C has to be sharpened to follow the pattern and also finish with a semitone.

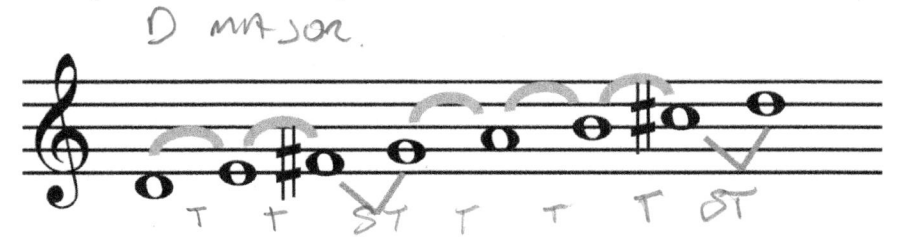

A Major

As we move around the Circle of Fifths, we will find more sharps.

From A to B there is a tone.

From B to C there is a semitone, but we need a tone, so we need to add a sharp to the C, which also makes a semitone to D.

From D to E there is a tone.

From E to F there is a semitone, but we need a tone, so we need to add a sharp to the F. This makes a semitone to G but we are looking for a tone so G should also be sharpened.

From G# to A there is a semitone so it fits.

F Major

From F to G there is a tone. From G to A there is a tone.

From A to B there is a tone but we need a semitone. How can we make a semitone from A to B? We just need to add a flat to the B.

Then from Bb to C we have a tone, so it works. C to D is a tone. D to E is a tone.

The last step from E to F is a semitone as the pattern requires.

Now, you might have this question: **"Why is it Bb and not A#?"** The reason why is easy: because if we named that note as A#, there will be two As in the scale (A natural and A sharp) and no Bs at all. This is incorrect because the scale would be missing one grade (IV) and it will be duplicating another one (III).

                        A   A#

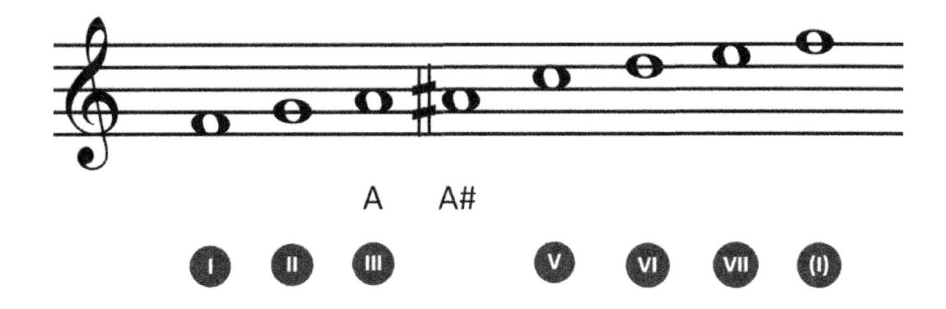

    ●   ●   ●   ●   ●   ●   ●
    I   II   III   V   VI   VII (I)

Let's continue with other scales:

Bb Major

If we move anticlockwise in the Circle of Fifths, the next step after F Major is Bb Major. Watch out that this scale, as its name suggests, starts and finishes on Bb.

From Bb to C there is a tone. From C to D there is a tone.

From D to E there is a tone but we need a semitone. How can we make a semitone from D to E? We just need to add a flat to the E.

Then from Eb to F we have a tone, so it works. F to G is a tone. G to A is a tone.

The last step from A to Bb is a semitone as the pattern requires.

Eb Major

All scales that are named "something flat major/minor" will start on a flat.

From Eb to F there is a tone.

From F to G there is a tone.

From G to A there is a tone but we need a semitone. We need to add a flat to the A.

From Ab to B there is a tone and a half! This is definitely too big. In order to reduce this distance to a tone, we need to make the B flat.

From Bb to C there is a tone, no problem.

From C to D there is a tone, thanks God!

From D to Eb there is a semitone. Done!

It is not a coincidence that these sharps or flats added in the major scales are the same that the keys have in their key signature, so in G Major the F needed to be sharp and in D Major, it was the F and the C the ones that needed to be adjusted.

On the other hand, no sharps or flats are needed to make the major scale pattern of tones and semitones in the key of C Major, so the key signature for C Major has no sharps or flats.

Scales can be written using any clef. At this level, you need to know how to write C Major, G Major, D Major, A major, F Major, Bb Major and Eb Major scales in bass clef.

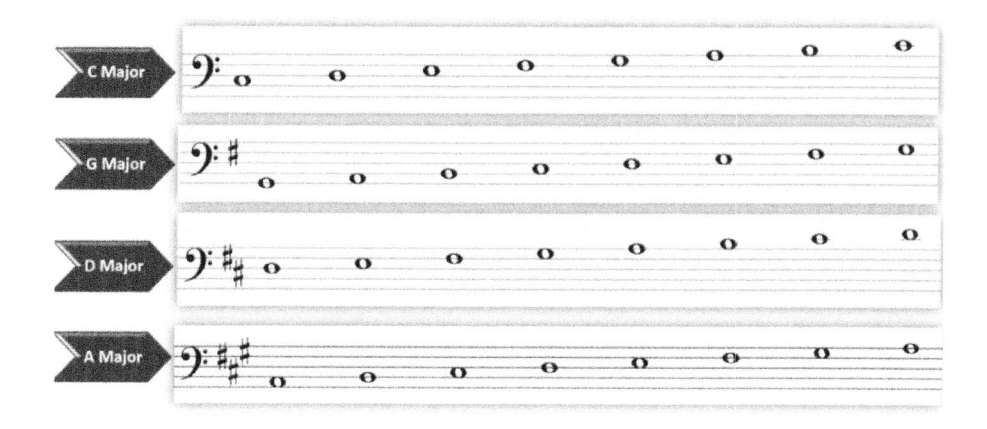

[F Major scale in bass clef]

[Bb Major scale in bass clef]

[Eb Major scale in bass clef]

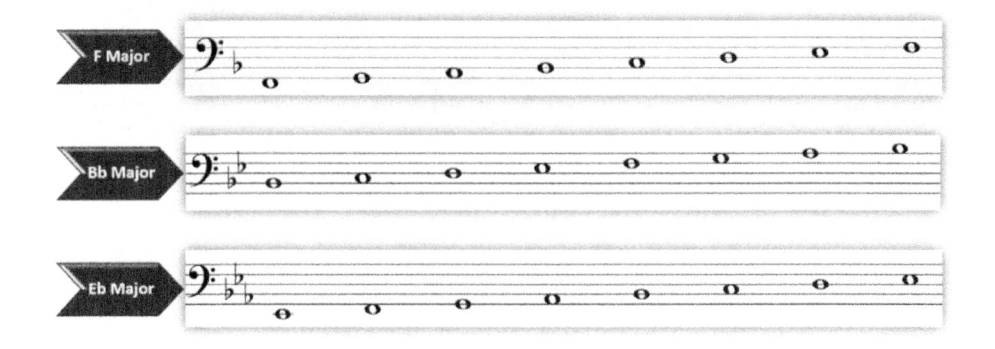

Descending Major Scales

All the previous examples have been ascending scales, but scales can be descending as well. To make a descending scale, we need to reverse the pattern:

Semitone – tone – tone - tone – Semitone – tone – tone

St T T T St T T

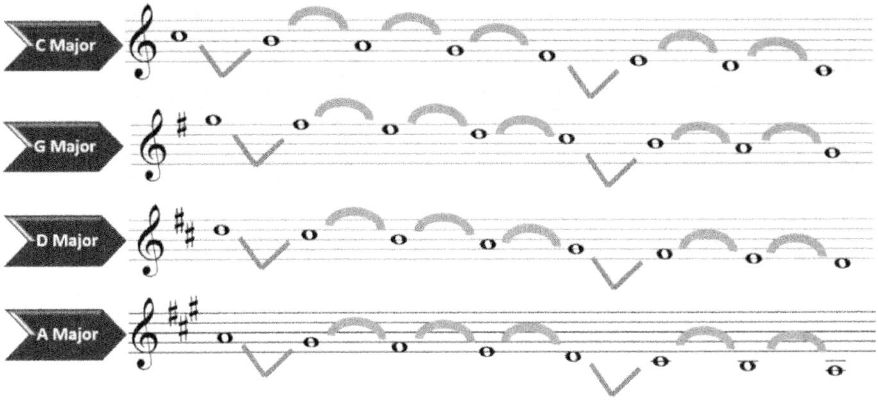
C Major
G Major
D Major
A Major

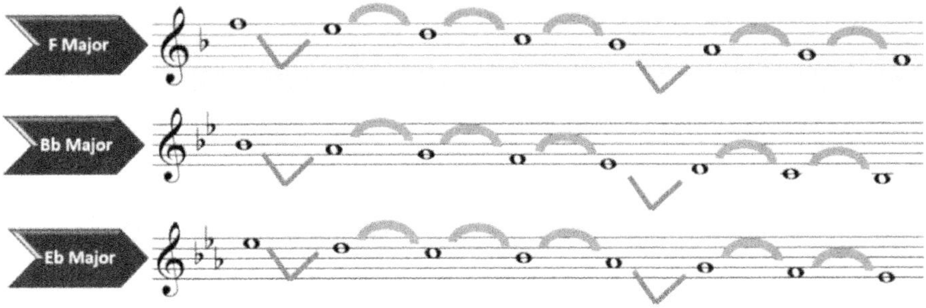
F Major
Bb Major
Eb Major

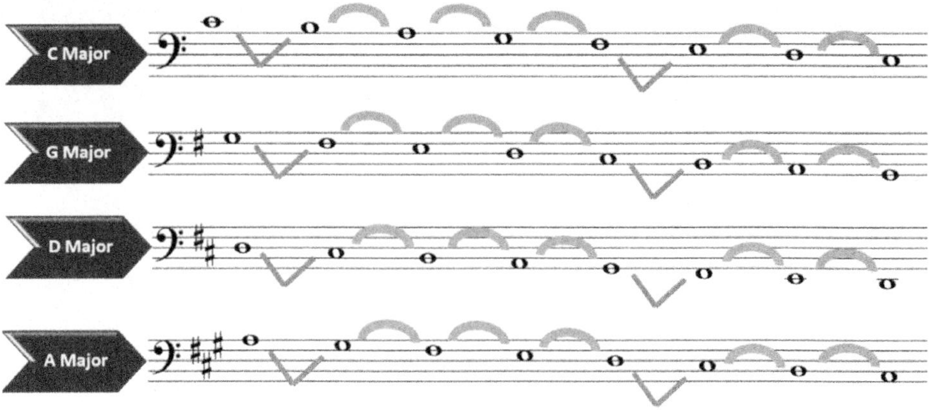
C Major
G Major
D Major
A Major

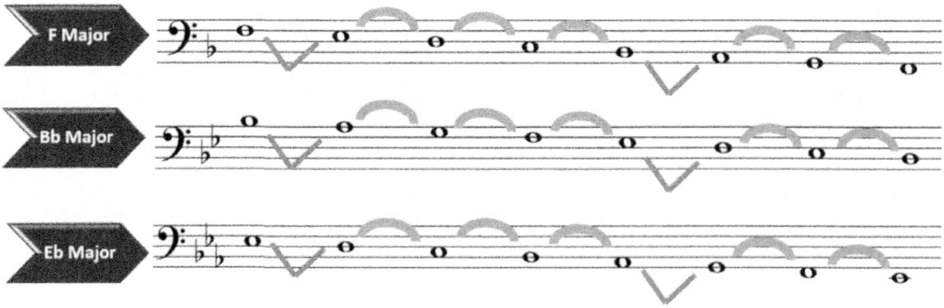
F Major
Bb Major
Eb Major

Degrees

Each note of the scale has a special name: degree.

Within any key, major or minor, the first degree of the scale (whatever the octave) is called **Tonic**, First Degree or **key-note**. Tunes often begin and end on it with the result that the tonic sounds special.

Degrees are represented by Roman numbers.

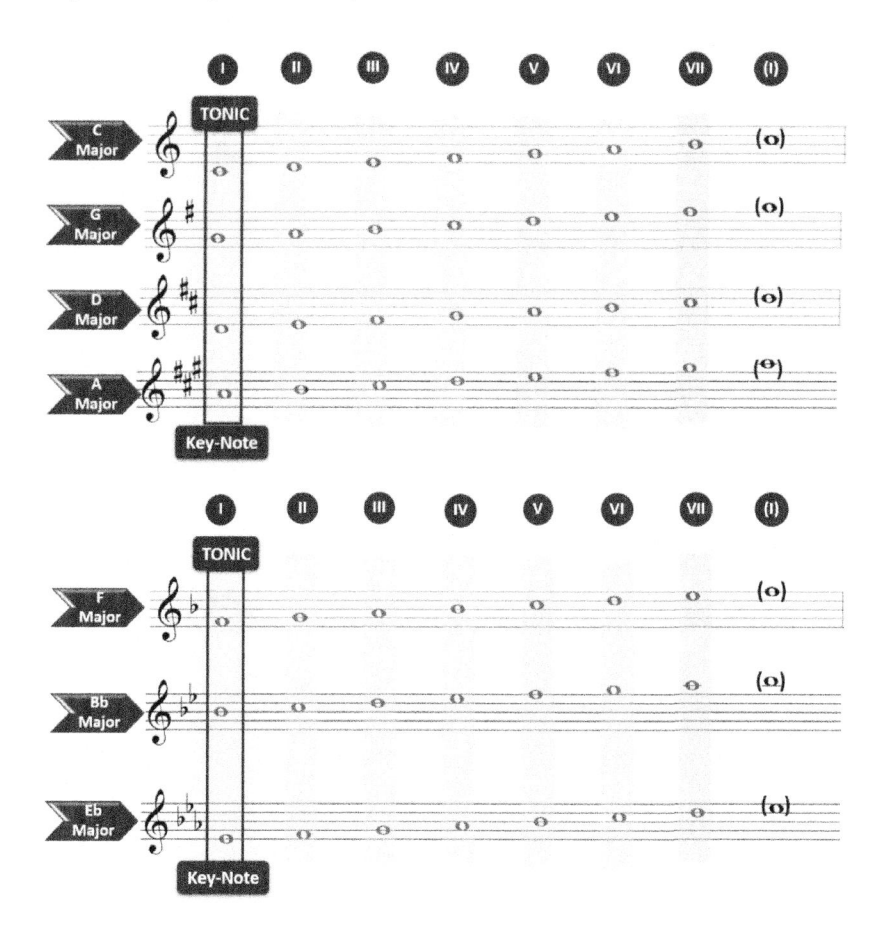

Minor scales

After major scales, the next most common in western classical music are the minor scales.

In Grade 1 you learned that in any major scale, semitones appear only between the III-IV and the VII-VIII degrees of the scale. Minor scales sound different from major scales mainly because **the tone-semitone pattern is different.**

In Grade 2, you need to learn A minor, E minor and D minor.

There are three types of minor scales, each of them having its own characteristics:

Natural minor

This is the easiest. The pattern of tones and semitones is:

Ascending: T-S-T-T-S-T-T and descending (same but backwards)

Watch out that **the semitones fall between the II-III and the V-VI degrees of the scale.**

Natural minor

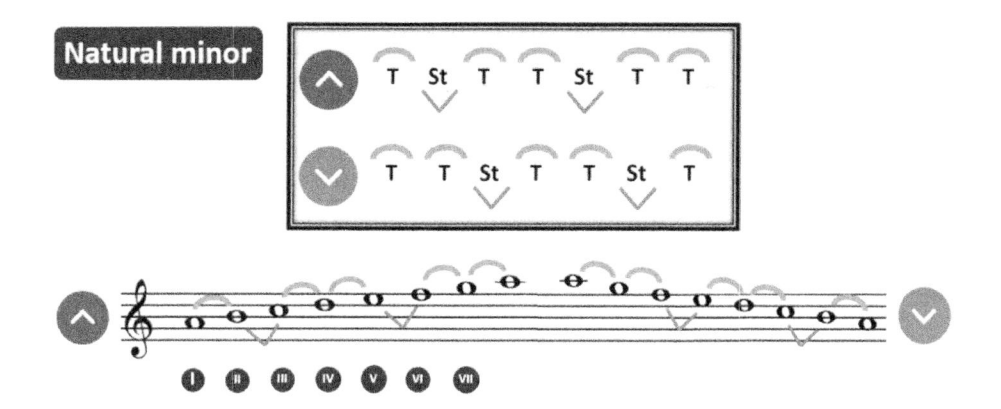

Harmonic minor

The harmonic scale is the same as the natural minor scale except that the **VII degree is raised by a semitone** (in both, ascending and descending scales). This will result in a tone and a half between the VI and VII degrees and semitones between the II and III, the V and VI and the VII and VIII. So, then the pattern will be T-S-T-T-S-T+ST-S. And backwards for the descending scale.

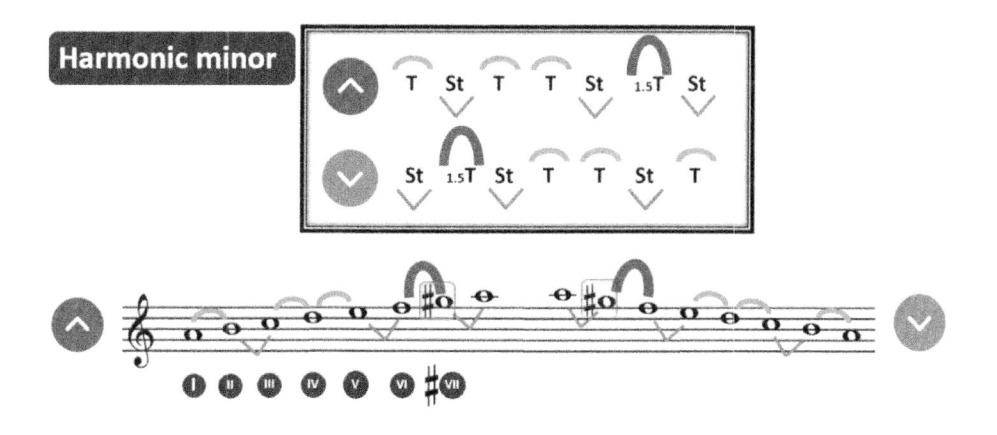

Harmonic minor

Melodic minor

This is the most sophisticated of the three, as it **raises the VI and VII grades when ascending, but cancels these when descending.**

It is easier to understand with examples:

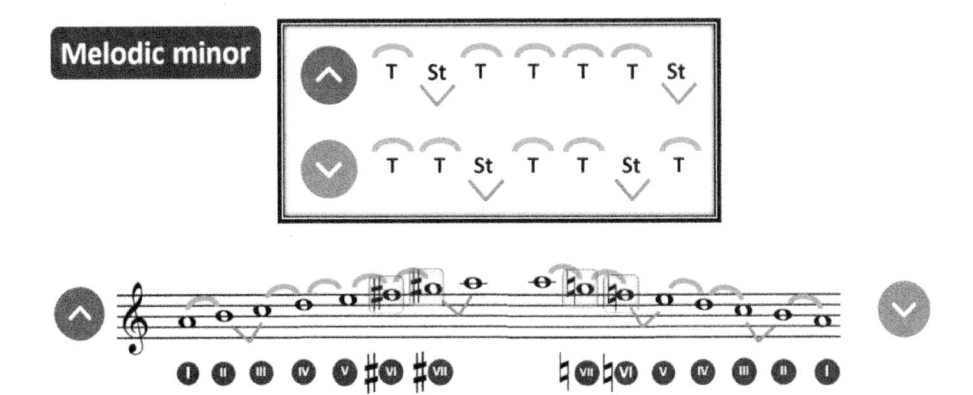

Grade 2 minor scales

A minor

First of all, **double check what is the key signature** of your scale. A minor has no sharps or flats, so the A minor natural scale will look like this:

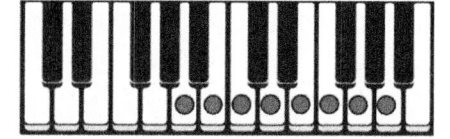

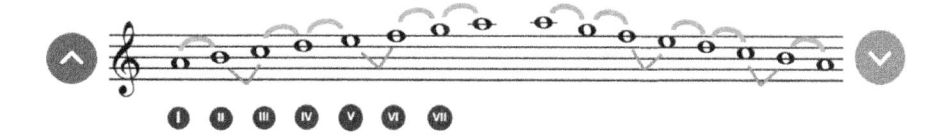

To continue with the harmonic scale, ask yourself, what is the seventh grade in the scale? G. So G will need to be sharpened in order to be raised by a semitone.

A Harmonic minor

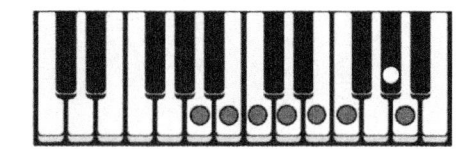

For the melodic scale, the VI and VII grades need to be raised by a semitone, so F and G will become sharp on the way up. These sharps are cancelled on the way down and F and G are played natural.

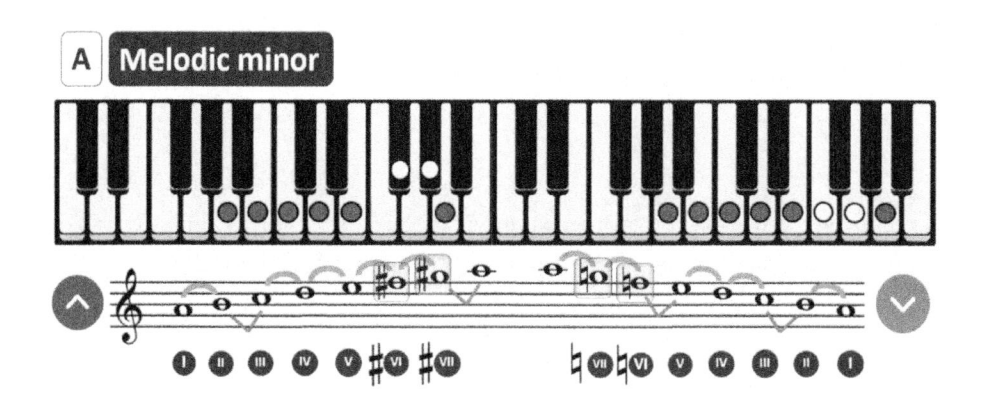

A Melodic minor

E minor

Let's have a look now to the E minor scales.

E minor has one sharp (F#) in the key signature, **don't forget to write** that next to the clef and before the time signature.

E minor natural goes from E to E, passing through the F# given in the key signature.

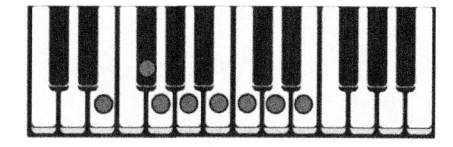

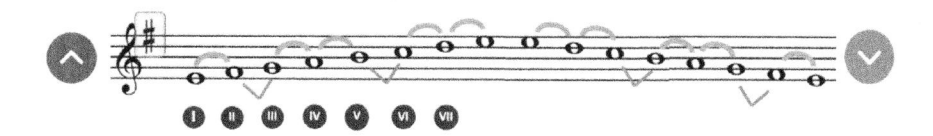

E minor harmonic will have the F# plus D#.

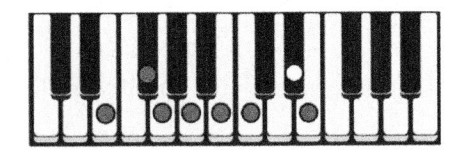

E Harmonic minor

E minor melodic will have F# plus C# and D# on the way up. Pay attention that C and D will be natural on the way down but the **F remains # because it is given in the key signature.**

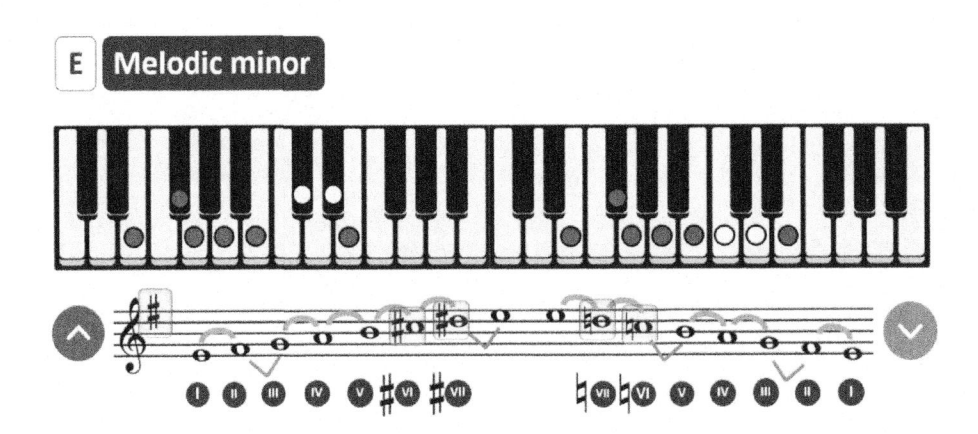

E Melodic minor

D minor

The last scale we will work on is D minor. Its relative major is F Major and the key signature is one flat. (Bb)

D minor natural goes from D to D, passing through Bb.

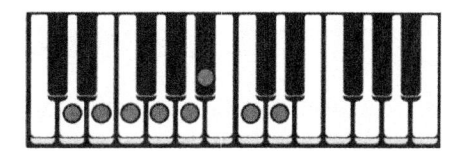

D Natural minor

D minor harmonic has Bb plus C#. Note that we used **C# and not Db**. This is because if we called that sound Db, we will have two Ds (Db and D natural) and no Cs. The only way to keep the C and raise it by a semitone is adding a # to it.

D Harmonic minor

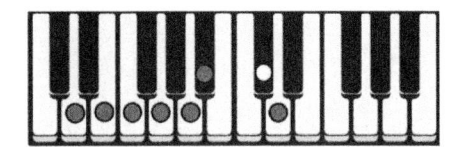

In D minor melodic we raise the VI and VII degrees by a semitone, so will only have a C# on the way. The VI and VII degrees get back to normal on the way down so we will only have a Bb when descending.

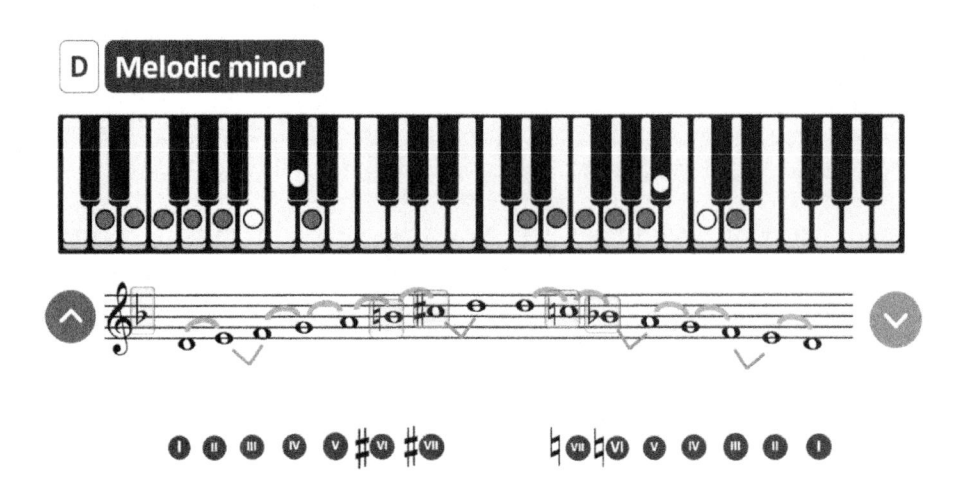

D Melodic minor

But you may ask, "**Didn't you say we could not mix sharps and flats?**" Yes, we said so, but **that rule applies to key signatures only. Not to scales.** Actually, it will get quite mixed up and will even have double accidentals as you progress with your music theory.

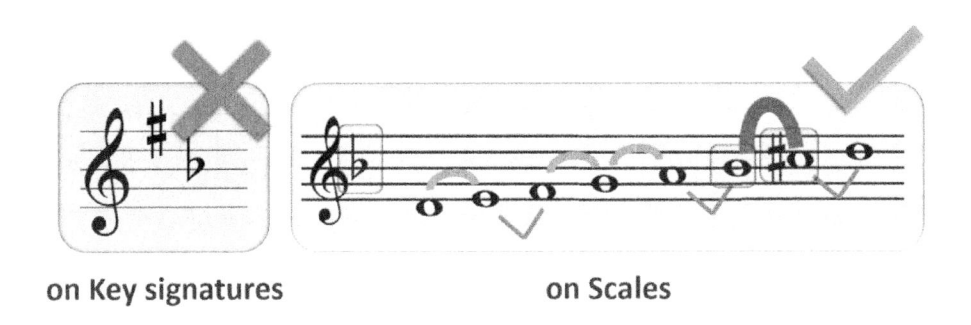

on Key signatures   on Scales

Attention! The terms natural, harmonic and melodic refer only to scales, not to keys. For example, **a piece of music cannot be in the key of "A minor harmonic" or "A minor melodic"**. Even though the notes of the harmonic and melodic scales may be easily recognized, the key of the piece will **just be named as A minor.**

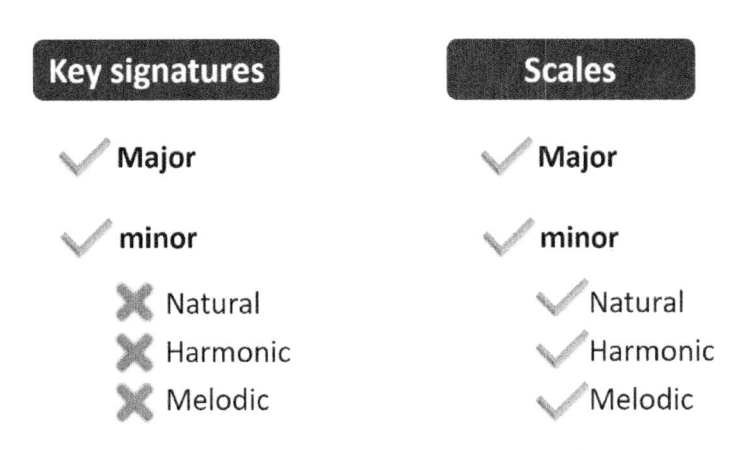

Key signatures	Scales
✓ Major	✓ Major
✓ minor	✓ minor
✗ Natural	✓ Natural
✗ Harmonic	✓ Harmonic
✗ Melodic	✓ Melodic

As discussed with the major scales, you should also be able to write all minor scales ascending, descending and in other clefs:

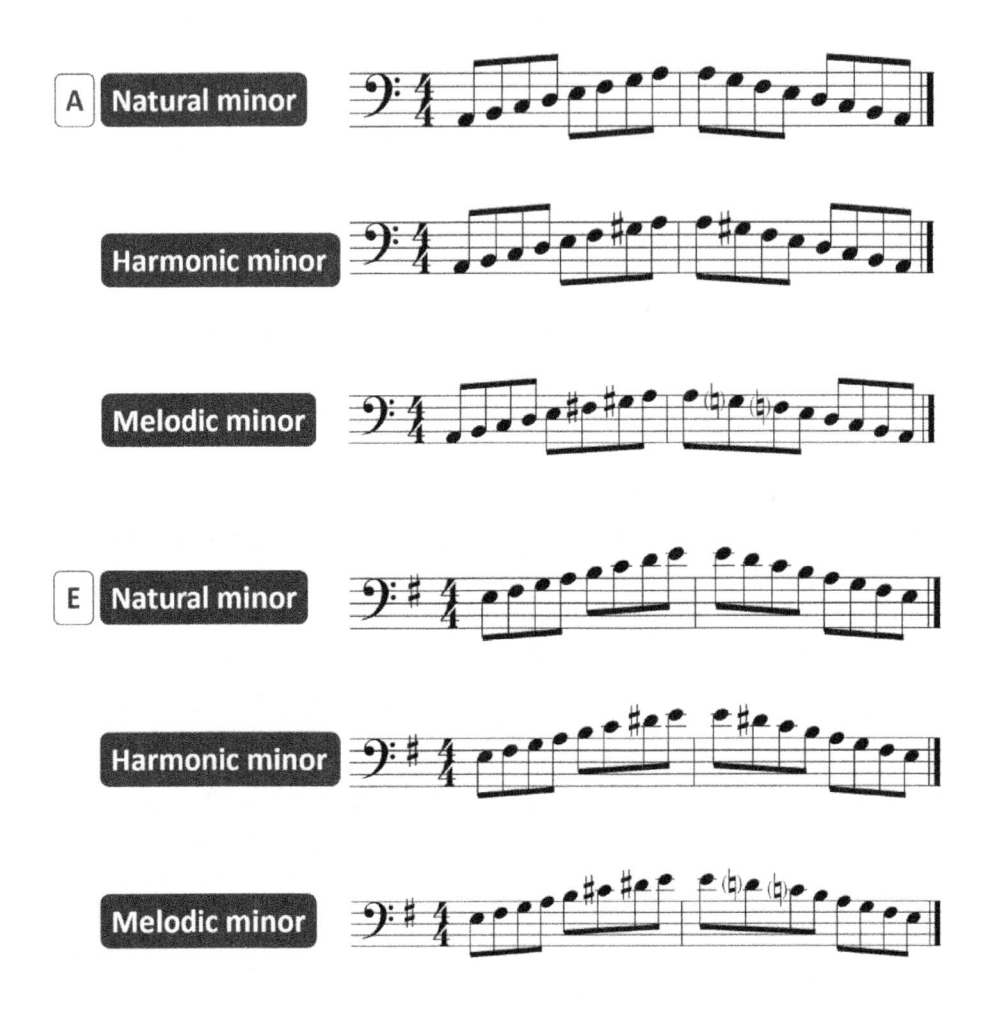

A Natural minor

Harmonic minor

Melodic minor

E Natural minor

Harmonic minor

Melodic minor

D **Natural minor**

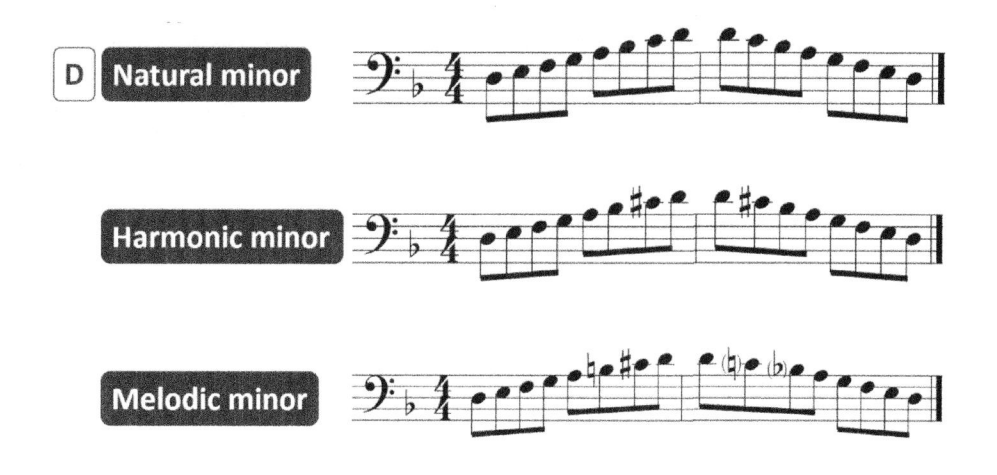

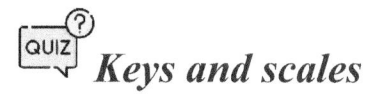

Harmonic minor

Melodic minor

Keys and scales

https://forms.gle/Kz87kQ2r8o2MXb7BA

Chords

A chord is a group of two or more **notes played at the same time**.

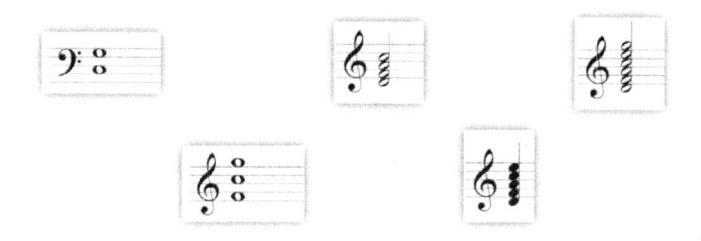

Tonic Triad

In classical music, the tonic triad is one of the chords most frequently used. It is made up of the I, III and V degrees of the scale.

If we look at the scale of C Major and put the I, III and V degrees together, we will find that the tonic triad chord is made of C, E and G.

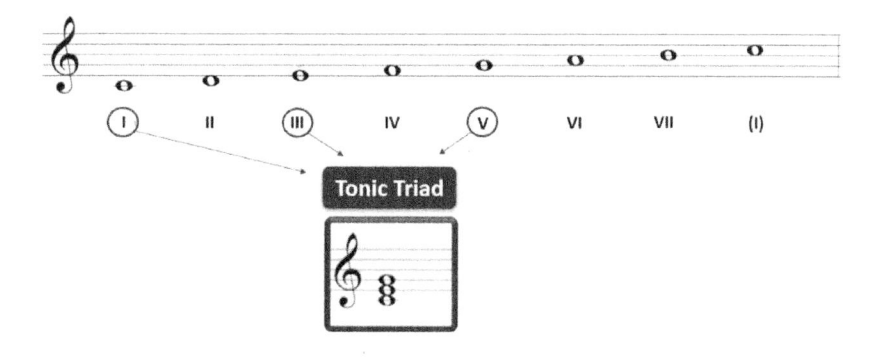

Any other tonic triad in other keys can be worked out the same way, so:

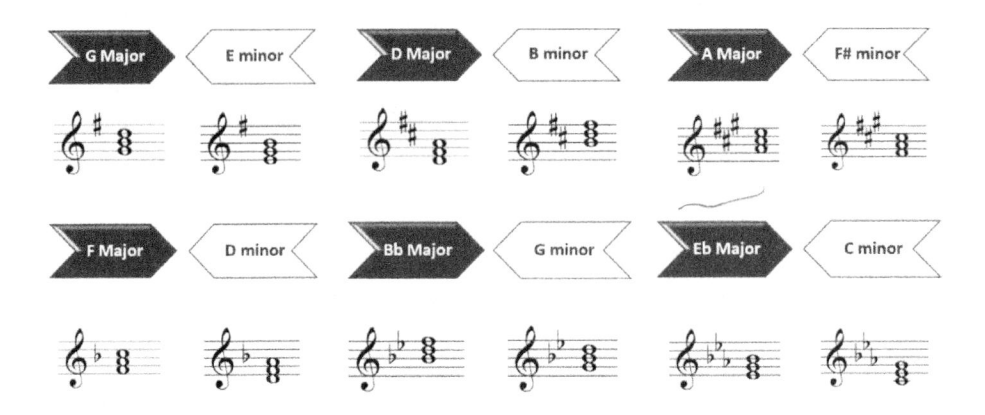

G Major	E minor	D Major	B minor	A Major	F# minor

F Major	D minor	Bb Major	G minor	Eb Major	C minor

In some music scores, chords are written with a different nomenclature. You will learn many chords and how to label them in the future. In Grade 2, you only needed to know that **the tonic triad can be represented as 'I' or just by the letter of the key-note**. For example, as a C for the C Major tonic triad.

At this stage, you should also know that minor chords can also be labeled as 'i' or by the letter of the key-note followed by **a lower case 'm'**. This shows that the chord is still built on the I degree of the scale but it contains the minor third.

Chords

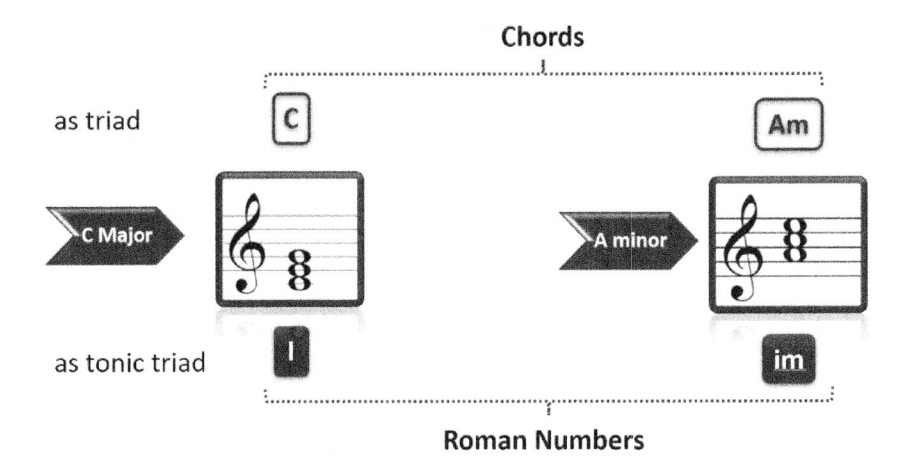

as triad   C   Am

C Major   A minor

as tonic triad   I   im

Roman Numbers

Watch out! **Write Roman numerals below the stave but chord symbols above it.**

The stems on a high chord should point downwards and stems on a low chord should point upwards.

Stems on a low chord   Stems on a high chord

Chord inversions

A chord (for example, the tonic triad) will always be formed of the same notes. However, **they can be written in different order.** Depending on which note is at the bottom, the chord is said to be in root position or an inversion.

Root position: When chords are written with the **tonic** (also called **root**) **at the bottom**, they are said to be in root position. Here is a tonic triad in C major in root position.

First Inversion: When the chord has the third at the bottom. Here is a tonic triad in C major in first inversion.

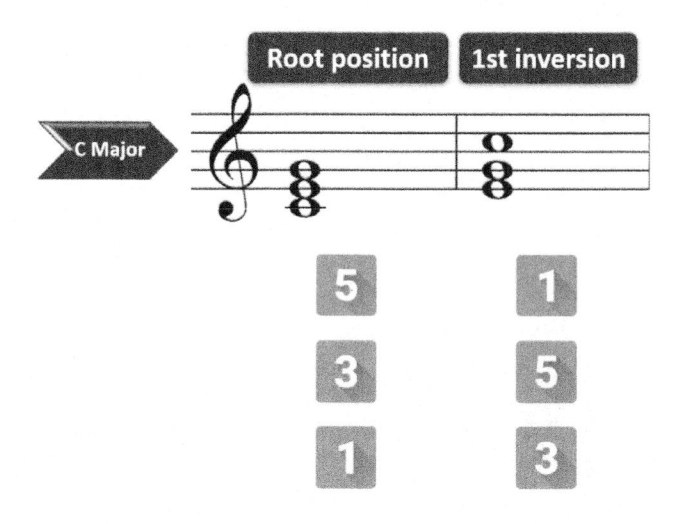

Arpeggios

An arpeggio is a sequence of notes made by **breaking up a chord** and playing it note after note as a melody. Arpeggios can be ascending (going up) or descending (going down).

Here is how the tonic triad one octave arpeggio would look like in the keys we have learned so far:

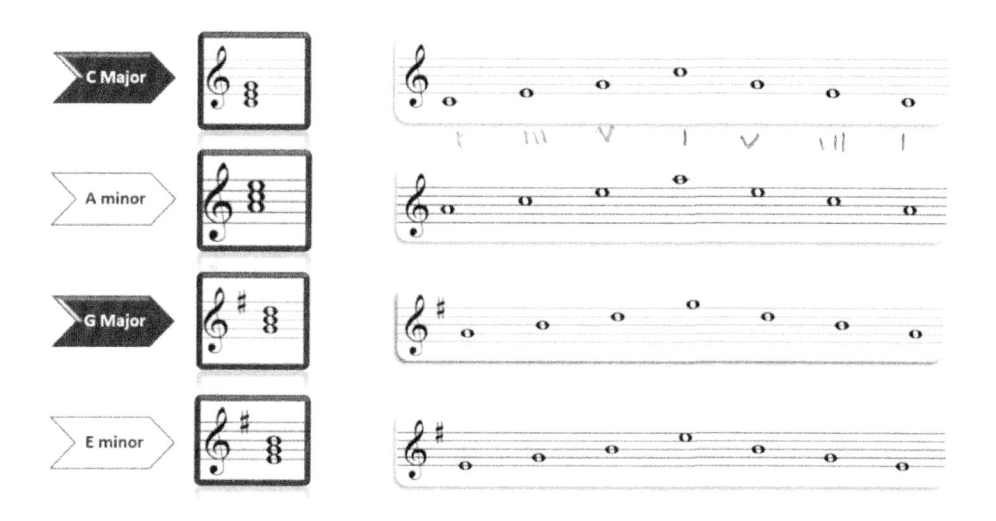

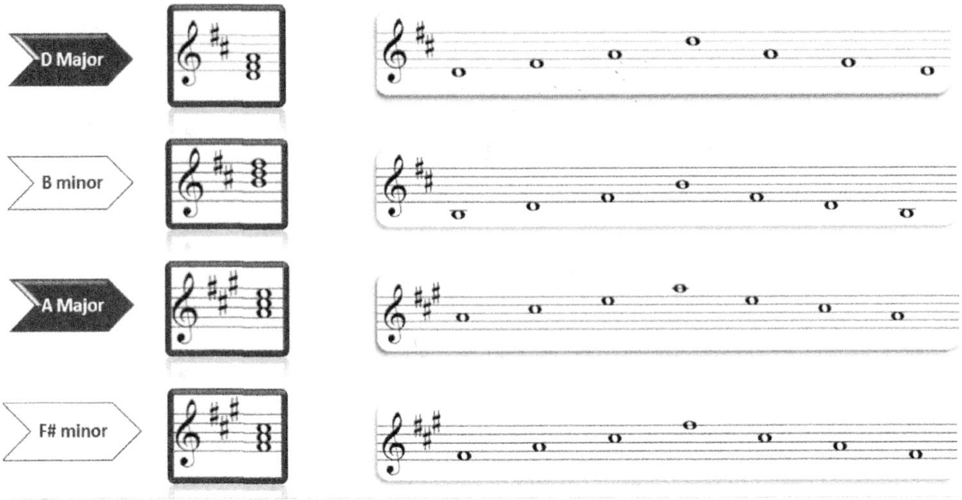
D Major
B minor
A Major
F# minor

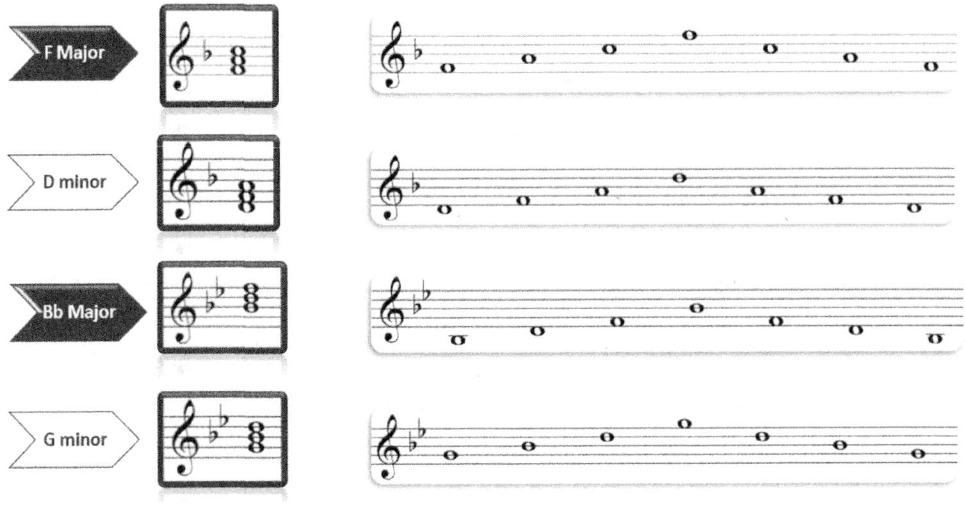
F Major
D minor
Bb Major
G minor

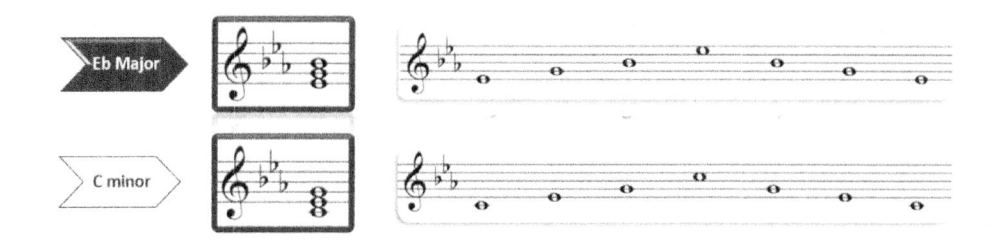

Broken chords

Like an arpeggio, a broken chord is made by literally breaking up a chord. They are used to give music different textures and to make accompaniments sound more interesting.

The difference between an arpeggio and a broken chord is that an arpeggio will not change direction; it will either go up or down in one go.

The broken chord is usually a longer sequence made of inner arpeggios. Sometimes we can find one-octave arpeggios within larger broken chord patterns.

Look at these examples:

Each group of semiquavers forms an individual ascending arpeggio in G Major. However, the first group starts on G, the second on B and the third on D. Aren't these the three notes of the G Major tonic triad? This is the reason why they are called broken chords.

There are lots of ways of making broken chords, depending on the rhythm used and how many notes are there in each pattern.

Here are other examples using the tonic triad in the key of G Major:

Tonic Triad

https://forms.gle/Uh8XCh5E8BJ7VHCz6

Intervals

An interval is the **distance between two notes**, whether played simultaneously or one after the other.

There are two types of intervals: harmonic and melodic.

Harmonic and Melodic

When the two notes sound simultaneously, the interval is called harmonic. If the notes are played one after the other, the interval is named as melodic.

Measuring Intervals by number

The size of an interval can be measured by number and quality, but in this level, we will only work on the number.

To measure an interval by number, we need to count the number of degrees of the scale that it includes. The number of degrees is the number of the interval.

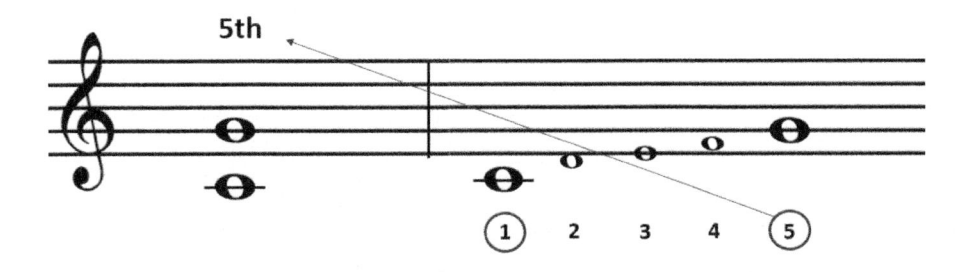

For example, from C to G there are five degrees, so the number of the interval is a fifth. Watch out that the given notes need to be counted too!

To describe intervals, we use ordinal numbers: 2nd, 3rd, 4th... and count upwards always from the lower note.

Look at these other examples:

From C to D, there are two degrees of the scale (I and II) so the interval is called a 2nd.

From C to E, there are three degrees of the scale (I, II and III) so the interval is called a 3rd

From C to F, there are four degrees of the scale (I, II, III and IV) so the interval is called a 4th.

It works the same way with the rest of the intervals.

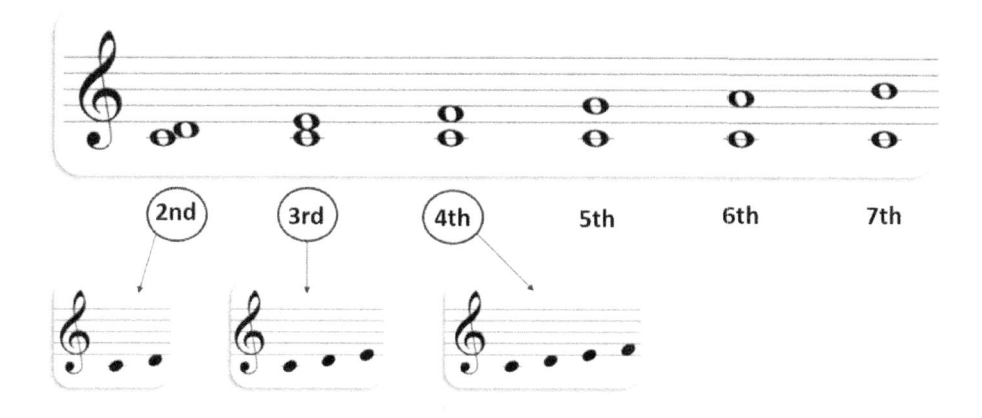

Intervals and Accidentals

Remember that a sharp or flat in any of the notes does not make any difference to the **interval number**. All these intervals for example, are 5ths because the amount of degrees that can fit between D and A is always five. They will be different in quality, but that is something you will learn in the next level.

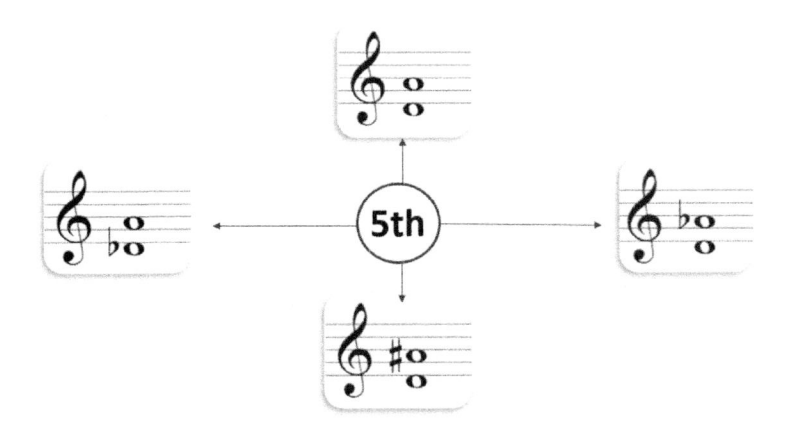

Unison and Octave

There are two intervals that are not usually known by the number:

Unison — where both notes have the same pitch

Octave — the distance between a note and the next note with the same letter name.

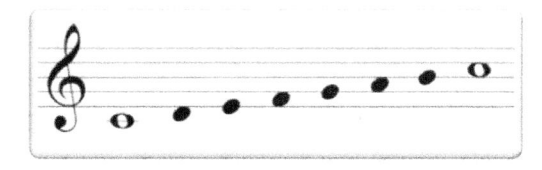

Grade 2 Intervals

These are all the intervals to learn at this stage. A tip to help you recognize them is that unisons, 3rds, 5ths and 7ths will have both notes either on lines or in spaces, while 2nds, 4ths, 6ths and octaves will have one note on a line and the other one in a space.

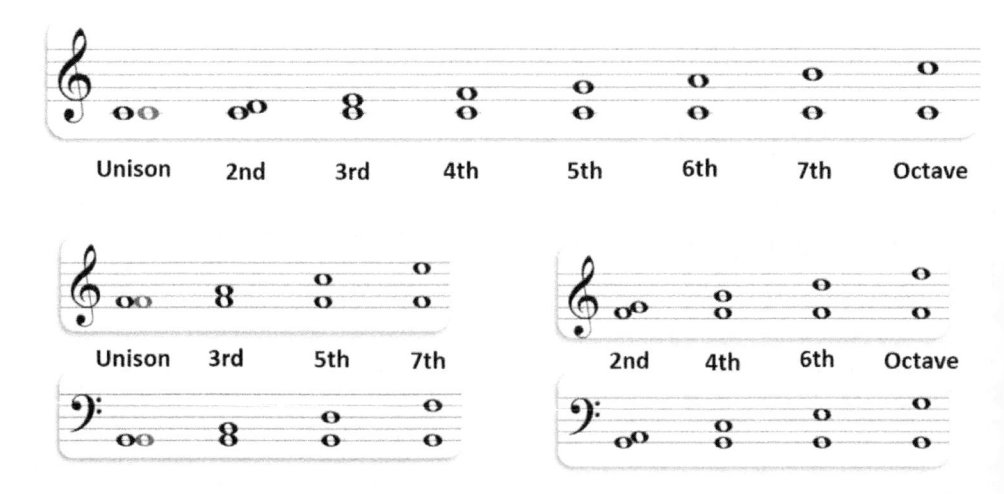

Measuring intervals by quality

Intervals can be classified by number and quality. We mentioned before that at this level, you will be working mainly on interval numbers, but you will also be introduced to some easy concepts about the quality of 2nd, 3rd, 4th, 5th and octaves. There will be many options to describe the quality of an interval. We will only talk about major, minor and perfect intervals:

Major and minor 2^{nds}

In every major and minor key there is always an interval of a major 2nd between the I and II degrees of the scale.

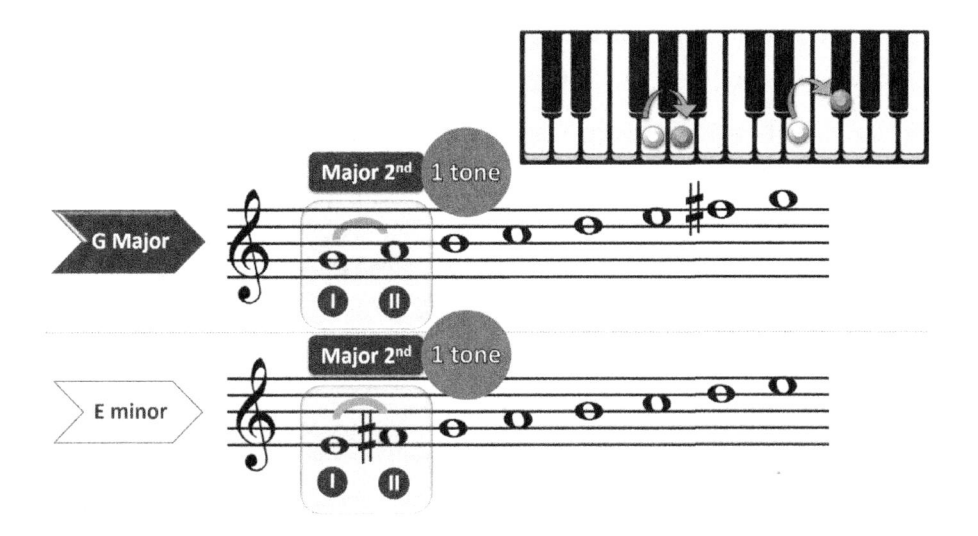

Major 2nds are formed of a tone (or two semitones) and are labelled as Major 2nd.

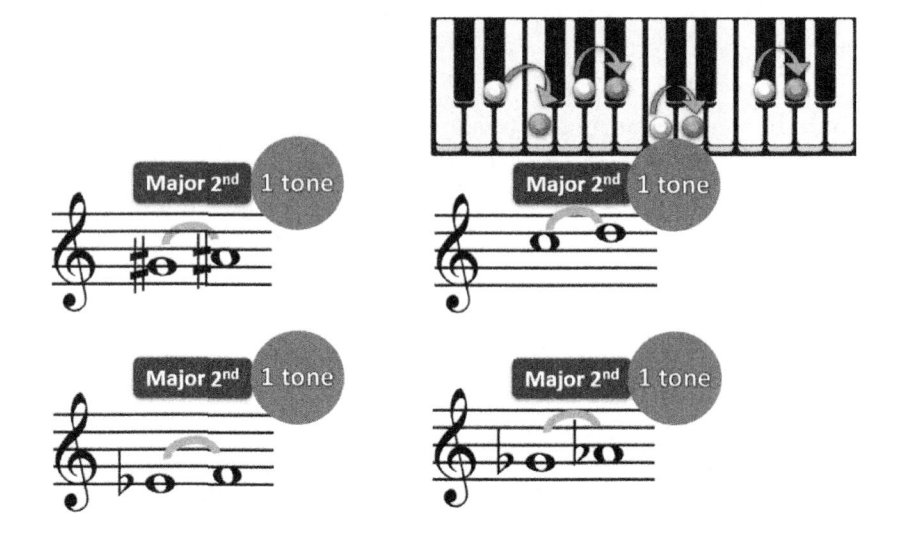

Minor 2nds are formed of a semitone and are labelled as Minor 2nd.

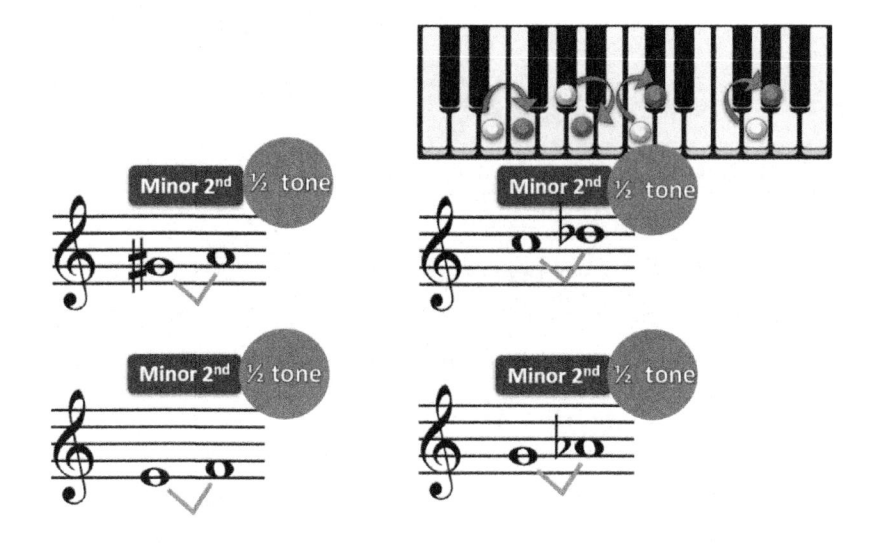

Major and minor 3rds

The third degree of a scale is the most obvious difference between the major and minor modes, and what gives the key a particular character.

In major keys, there is always an interval of a **major 3rd** between the I and III degrees of the scale.
Major 3rds are formed of two tones and labelled as 'Major 3rd'.

In minor keys there is always an interval of a **minor 3rd** between the I and III degrees of the scale. **Minor 3rds are formed of a tone and a half** (in other words, a tone and a semitone, or if you prefer, three semitones). They are labelled as 'Minor 3rd'.

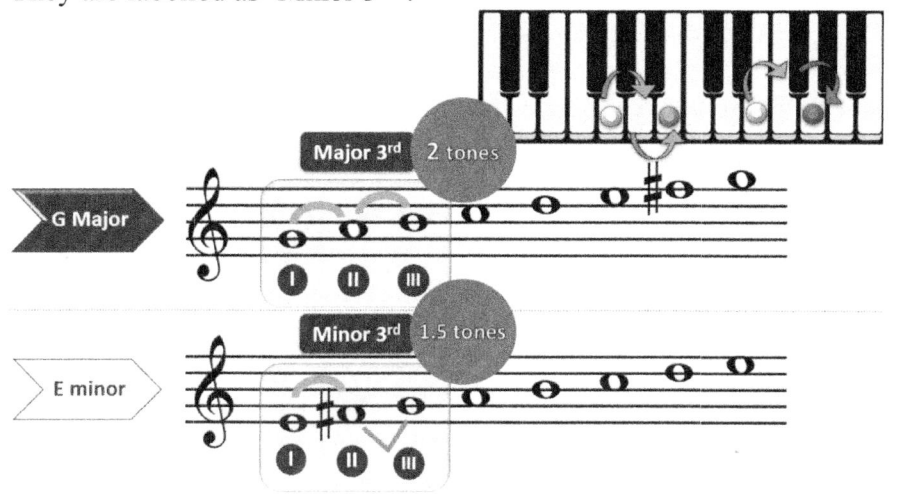

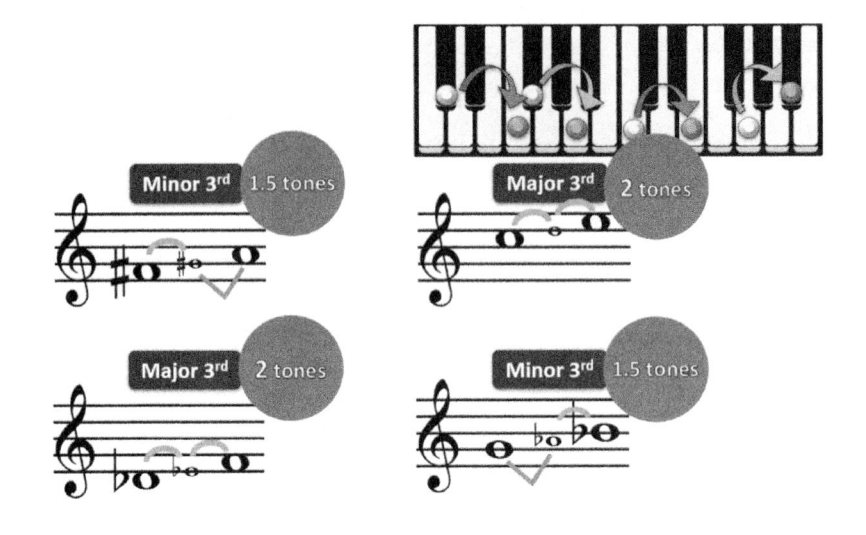

Perfect 4ths

All major and minor scales have a perfect 4th between the I and IV degrees of the scale.

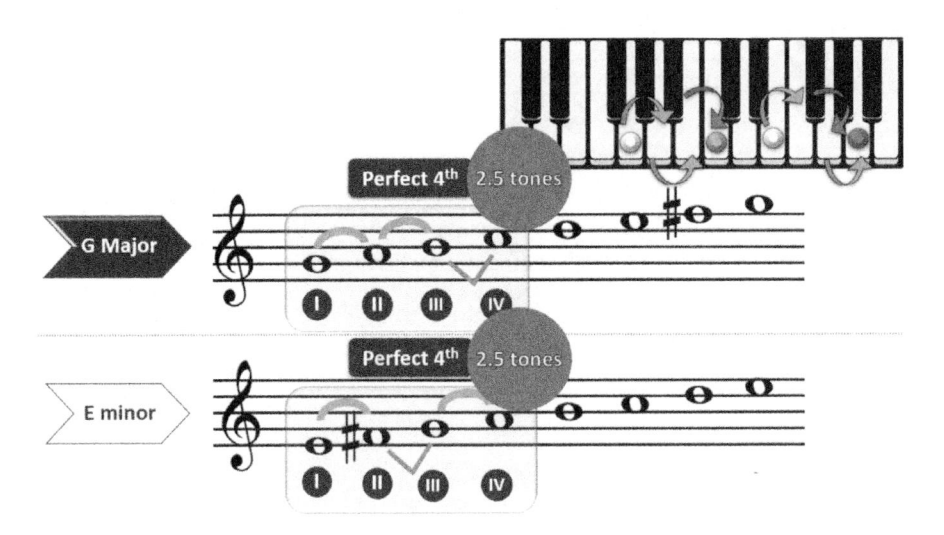

Perfect 5ths

A perfect 5th between the I and the V degrees of the scale.

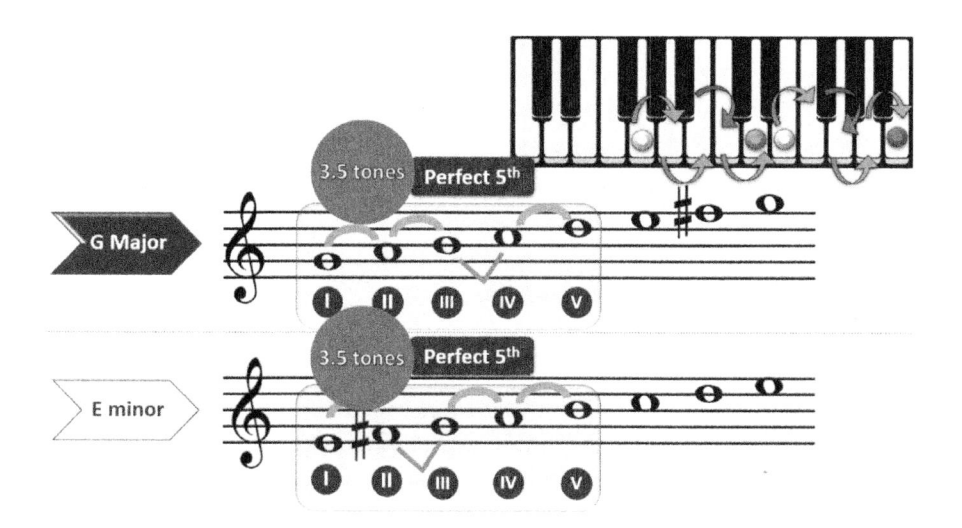

Octaves (8^{ves})

And a perfect octave (8^{ve}) from tonic to tonic. This means that all 4^{ths}, 5^{ths} and octaves that you find will be perfect in quality.

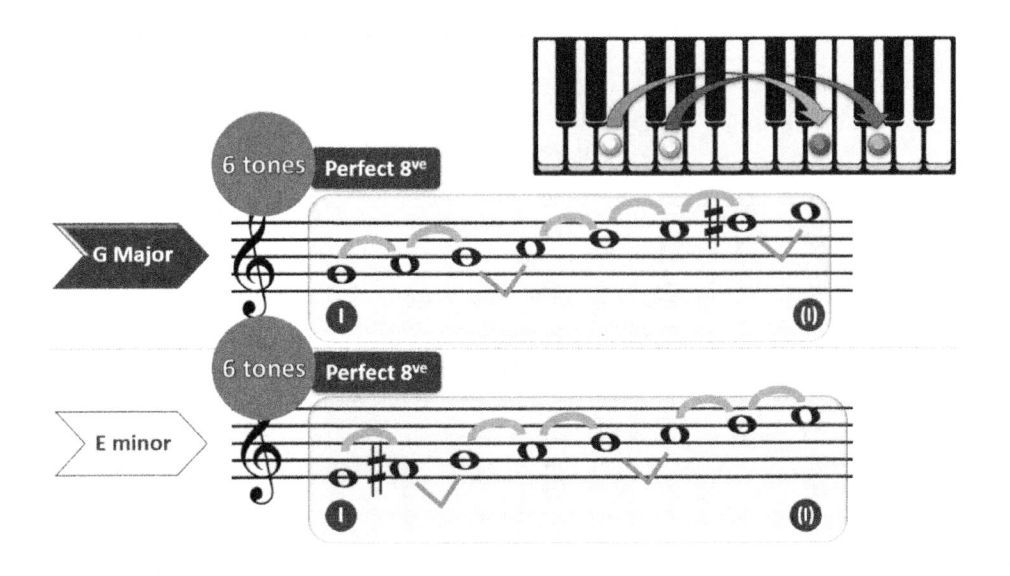

Intervals

https://forms.gle/qKMG6fJgW1Vwv1ZF9

Ostinato

An ostinato is **a pattern that is repeated persistently** in a piece of music. The repeated pattern could be a melody, a figure in the bass (called a basso ostinato) or simply a repeated rhythmic idea. An ostinato may be played for an entire piece of music or just during one short section. A famous example is Ravel's "Bolero", which uses the ostinato below played by the snare drum, all the way through the piece:

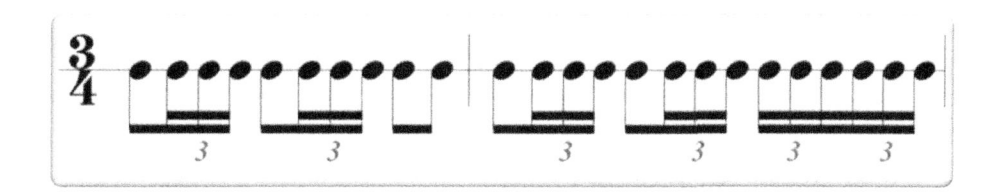

By the way! The plural of ostinato is ostinati.

Sequences

A sequence is a tune pattern that is repeated starting on a different note. Look at this example:

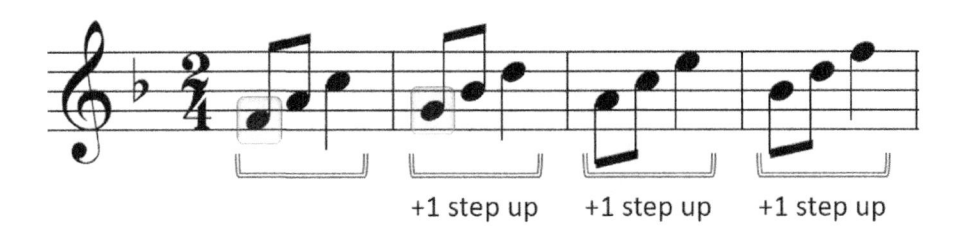

+1 step up   +1 step up   +1 step up

The second bar has the same tune pattern as the first but it is one note higher.

But then, what is the difference between an ostinato and a sequence? An ostinato repeats the rhythm to the same tune pattern. A sequence repeats the rhythm but also moves the pitch of the tune.

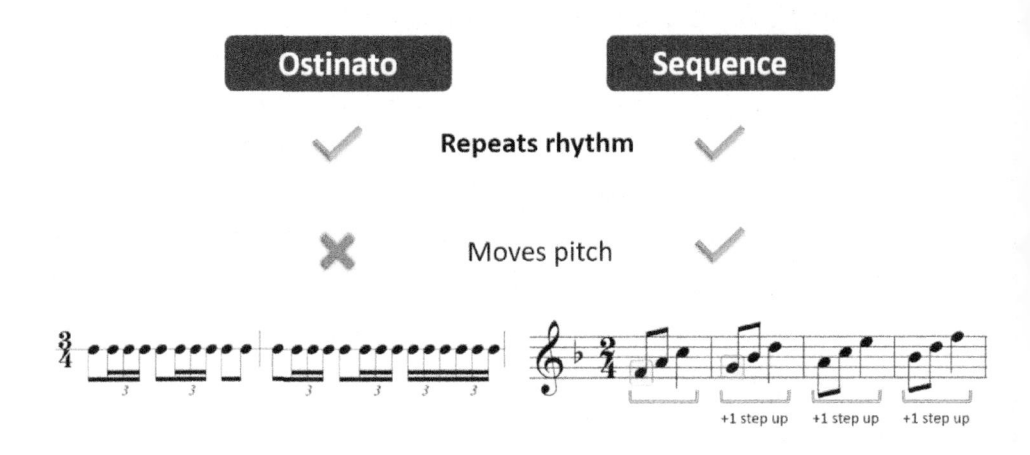

Ostinato		Sequence
✓	**Repeats rhythm**	✓
✗	Moves pitch	✓

Transposition

In certain circumstances, when music is hard to sight read or uncomfortable to sing, it is more convenient to write music in a different way. This could mean changing the octave, the clef or even the key signature. The process of applying these changes to rewrite and facilitate music is called transposition.

Let's start with an easy example to transpose this phrase up an octave: It may be very low for a soprano singer for example, so it is more comfortable to move it an octave higher.

However, the same excerpt may actually be too high for a male voice to sing. In this case, we would transpose the melody an octave lower.

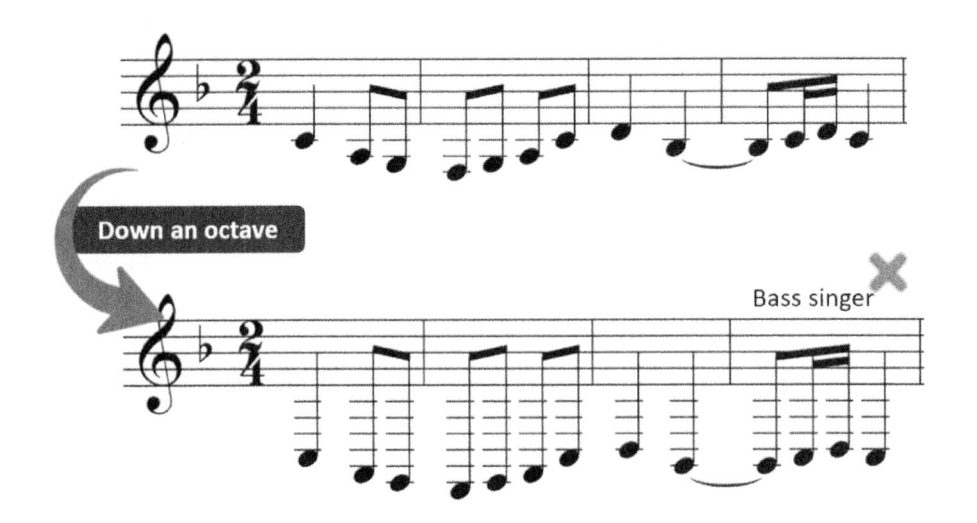

Watch out that the clef needs to be changed to bass clef to represent all these low sounds without so many ledger lines.

Performance Directions

Performance directions are instructions written by the composers to express their intention of how the music should be interpreted.

In other words, the performance directions are a range of musical terms to convey how composers want their music to be played. Understanding these helps musicians perform more accurately and within the proper style.

Either as full words or abbreviations, the language most often used for the performance directions is Italian, but we can also find German terms in some music.

They can be divided into six main categories:

- Dynamics
- Tempo
- Articulation
- Repeat marks
- Expression terms
- Other signs and terms.

Dynamics

Dynamics are signs that represent **how quiet or loud the music should be played**. From very soft to very loud, the dynamics most commonly used are:

Pianissimo   *Piano*   *Mezzo Piano*   *Mezzo Forte*   *Forte*   *Fortissimo*

$$pp \quad p \quad mp \quad mf \quad f \quad ff$$

Very Soft   Very Loud

In addition to the previous, we can also have **gradual changes of volume**, represented either as a hair-pin or with the actual word.

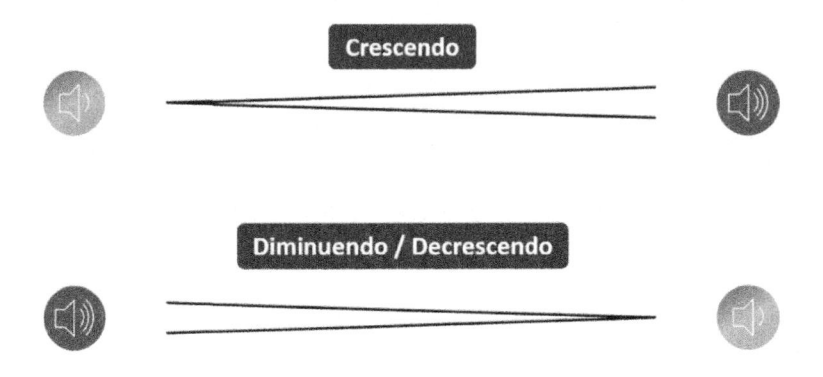

Crescendo

Diminuendo / Decrescendo

Another change of dynamic is *fp*, which stands for *fortepiano*. It means to play a particular note loud and then immediately soft. Specially used in wind or string instruments.

Tempo

Tempo Markings

The tempo of a piece of music is basically the **speed at which it should be played**.

From very slow to quick, the tempo marks you should know at this level are:

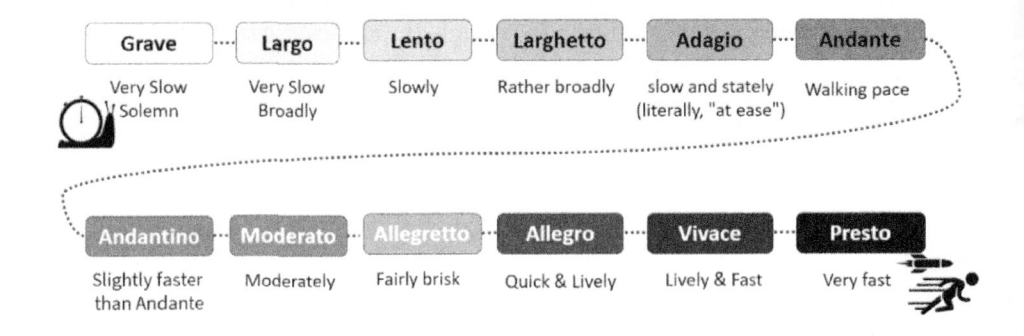

Grave	Largo	Lento	Larghetto	Adagio	Andante
Very Slow & Solemn	Very Slow Broadly	Slowly	Rather broadly	slow and stately (literally, "at ease")	Walking pace

Andantino	Moderato	Allegretto	Allegro	Vivace	Presto
Slightly faster than Andante	Moderately	Fairly brisk	Quick & Lively	Lively & Fast	Very fast

The tempo marks are written at the beginning, above the first bar, but can suddenly be changed if a new term is written throughout the piece.

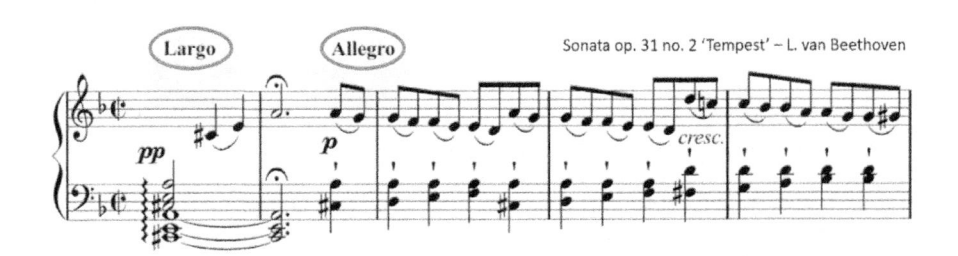

Another term related to tempo is *sostenuto*, which means sustained. It does not suggest a concrete speed, it expresses a rather held tempo in comparison with the previous one.

Tempo Changes

As with the dynamics, tempo can also have changes. The terms to name these changes in speed are:

Accelerando	Getting Faster
Rallentando	Slowing down (for emphasis)
Ritardando	Slowing down (holding back)
Ritenuto	Held Back
Allargando	Broadening, getting a little slower
A Tempo	Return to Original tempo

The terms "**poco**" or "**poco a poco**" mean little or little by little. They can be added to some tempo marks, for example: *Poco Adagio* or *Poco a Poco Accelerando*. In this excerpt, you would play a little rallentando.

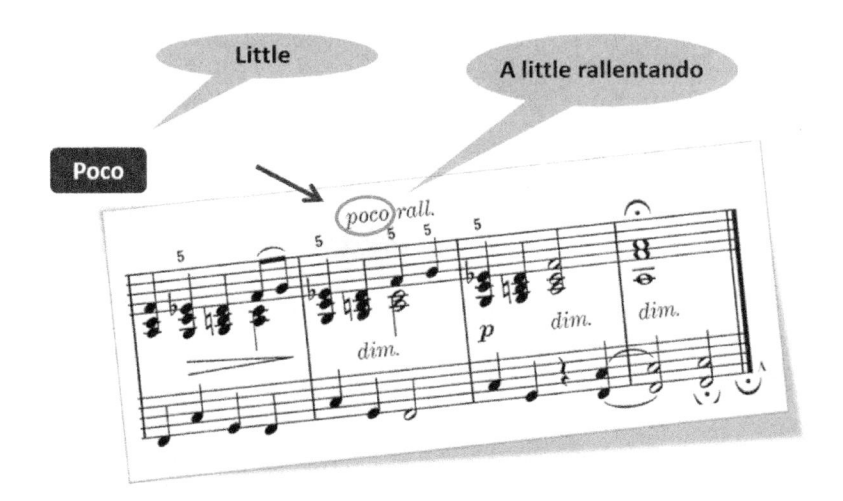

Metronome Marks

The metronome is an **instrument that makes repeated ticking sounds at an adjustable pace.**

The metronome marking at the beginning of a piece usually tells the player whether the speed of the beat (quaver, crotchet or minim) is slow or fast. A piece in 3/8 can be very slow if marked *Adagio*, while a piece in 2/2 can be very fast indeed if marked *Allegro molto*.

But… tempo marks can sometimes be very subjective or relative. For example, *Andante* means "play at a walking pace". Some of us may walk quicker or slower than others, so what would be the correct speed to play?

Many musicians have come across the same question since centuries ago. That is the reason why some composers use metronome markings to give the exact speed of the beat. These markings tell the player **how many quaver, crotchet or minim beats there are per minute.**

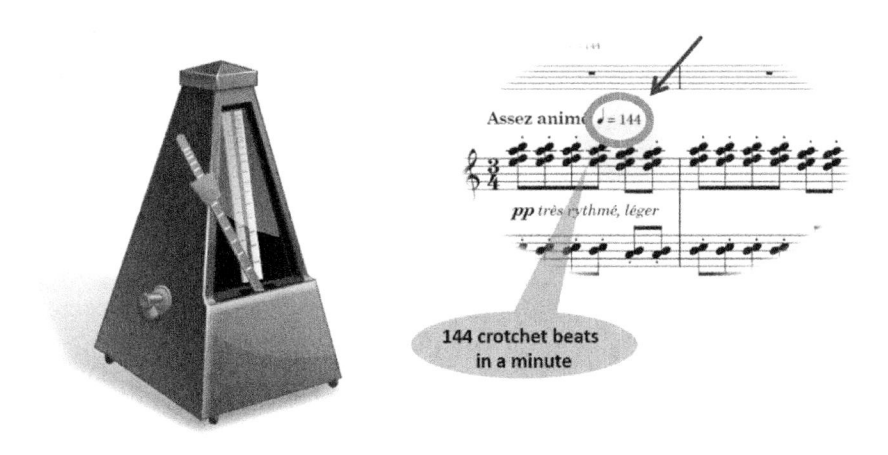

144 crotchet beats in a minute

For example, M.M. ♩ = 60, means that there will be 60 **crotchet** beats per minute. However, if we find the indication M.M ♩ = 60, it means that there will be 60 **minim** beats per minute. It could even be M.M. ♪ = 60, meaning that there will be 60 **quaver** beats per minute.

They are small indications that can make **huge differences in music**. Even though the number 60 remains the same, the fact that the beat changes from being a crotchet to being a minim, means that in the same time where I was playing only one crotchet before, I will need to squeeze two crotchets in. Music will become twice as fast.

On the other hand, if the metronome indicates ♪ = 60, it means that in the time where I was playing a crotchet before, now I only need half a crotchet. This is, a quaver. Music will become half slow.

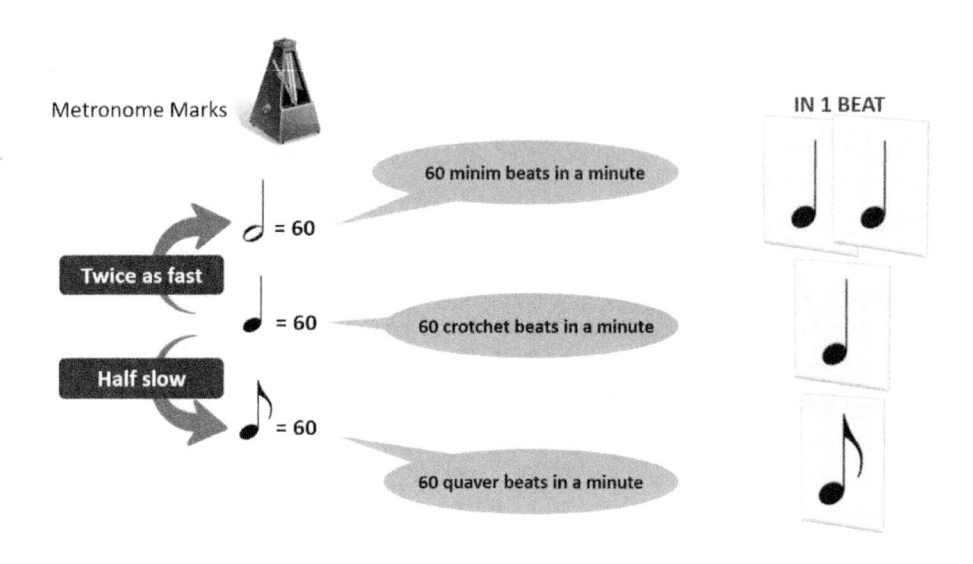

Metronome Marks

𝅗𝅥 = 60 — 60 minim beats in a minute

Twice as fast

♩ = 60 — 60 crotchet beats in a minute

Half slow

♪ = 60 — 60 quaver beats in a minute

IN 1 BEAT

𝅗𝅥 𝅗𝅥

♩

♪

188

Let's listen to / Try playing Twinkle Twinkle played with a metronome of ♩ = 60.

($♩ = 60$)

And now with a metronome of 𝅗𝅥 = 60.

($𝅗𝅥 = 60$) **Twice as fast**

And with a metronome of ♪ = 60.

($♪ = 60$) **Half slow**

Now, I would like you to look at these metronome marks:

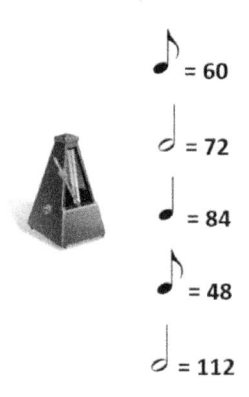

♪ = 60
𝅗𝅥 = 72
♩ = 84
♪ = 48
𝅗𝅥 = 112

What will be the fastest and slowest? As we have different values as the beat, it may not be so straight forward to tell.

If you need to compare speeds with different values, the best way is to **put all timings into the same type of beat.** For this, we need to do some maths: **when you move from quaver to crotchet, you need to divide the metronome number by 2. If you move from a minim to a crotchet, the operation is multiplying by 2.**

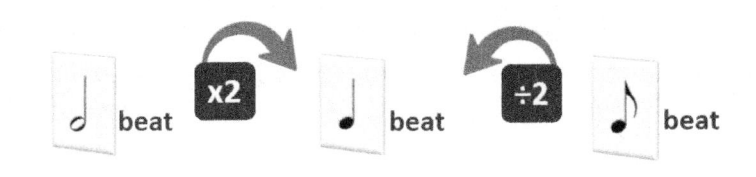

𝅗𝅥 beat **x2** ♩ beat **÷2** ♪ beat

Let's try to "translate" all these marking to crotchet beats:

- If ♪ = 60, the same speed represented with crotchets is ♩ = 30. Why? Because the quaver is the half of a crotchet, so I need to divide 60 by 2.
- The next one is 𝅗𝅥 = 72. The same speed represented with a crotchet beat will be ♩ = 144.
  Why? Because a minim is a double of a crotchet, so I need to multiply.
- ♪ = 48: Divide 48 by 2 and you will get that the crotchet beat is 24.
- 𝅗𝅥 = 112. Multiply by 2 and you will get that the crotchet beat is 224.

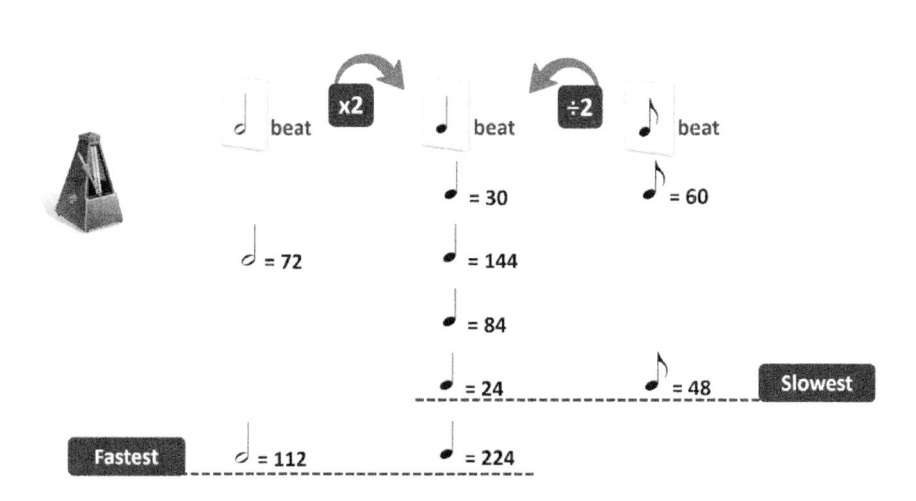

𝅗𝅥 beat x2 ♩ beat ÷2 ♪ beat

♩ = 30   ♪ = 60

𝅗𝅥 = 72   ♩ = 144

          ♩ = 84

          ♩ = 24   ♪ = 48   **Slowest**

Fastest 𝅗𝅥 = 112   ♩ = 224

Now that we know what the crotchet beat is on each of these metronome marks, we can put them in order and realize that $\eighth = 48$ was the slowest and $\half = 112$ the fastest.

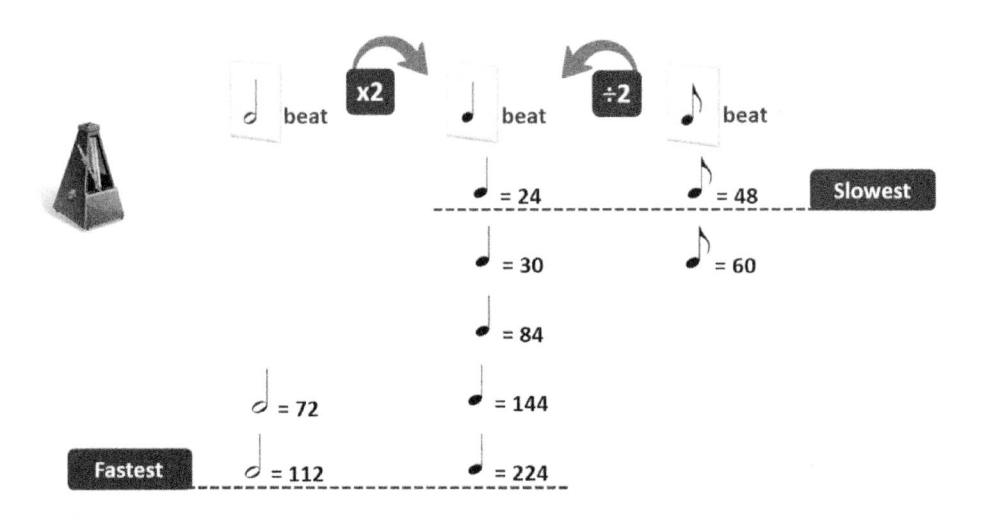

But then, you may ask: if I can find the crotchet beat of any metronome marking, why would composers ask me to feel the music in quavers of minims?

Well, answer yourself this question. Listen to a metronome beat in 24.

($\quarter = 24$)

Isn't it far too slow? Don't you get bored? In this case, it will be better to listen to 48 and consider that a quaver. The speed does not change and it is easier for players to practice.

($♪$ = 48)

($♩$ = 170)

On the other hand, listen to the metronome at 170.

Isn't it too noisy and annoying? Don't you get stressed out? Of course, you are hearing 170 ticks per minute. In this case, it will be better to listen to "only" 85 beats per minute and say they are minims.

($\quarternote$ = 85)

There were many inventors who experimented to create an apparatus to indicate tempo more precisely, but the metronome as we know it today was attributed to Johann Nepomuk Maelzel (1772-1838).

Metronome marks can be written with or without the abbreviation M.M., which stands for Maelzel's Metronome.

Johann Nepomuk Maelzel

Maelzel's Metronome

Beethoven, as scrupulous as he was in his work, was one of the first composers to include metronome marks in his pieces.

Articulation

The articulation symbols appear either above or below the notes and are used to describe **how a note should be played or sung**. There are many signs which represent detailed instructions, but at this level, we will only learn some of them.

Legato

Legato means linked or connected and represents smooth playing

195

Legato can also be written with slurs. These are curved lines which join a certain number of notes to represent smooth playing between them.

Slurs also indicate phrase lengths and places for singers to breath.

Staccato

Staccato is the Italian word for detached. It is represented by small dots above or below the head-note and means that the notes should be shortened.

Staccato

Play detached

Accent

Accents are small triangles written above or below the head-note that indicate the note should be played with a certain force.

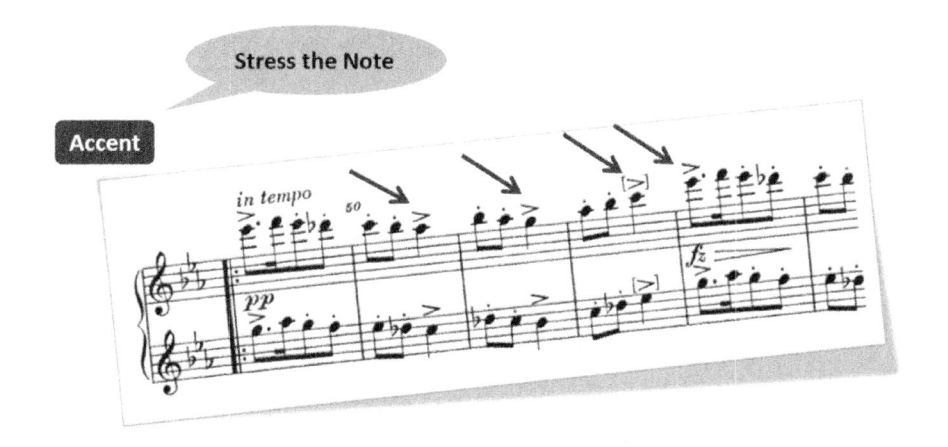

Stress the Note

The instructions of how to play each note can get more sophisticated as you progress in your instrument or voice. While legato and staccato are the most basic forms of articulation, there are others to learn:

Tenuto

It is a horizontal short line placed above or below the note to represent a heavier touch on the note and a separation to the next one.

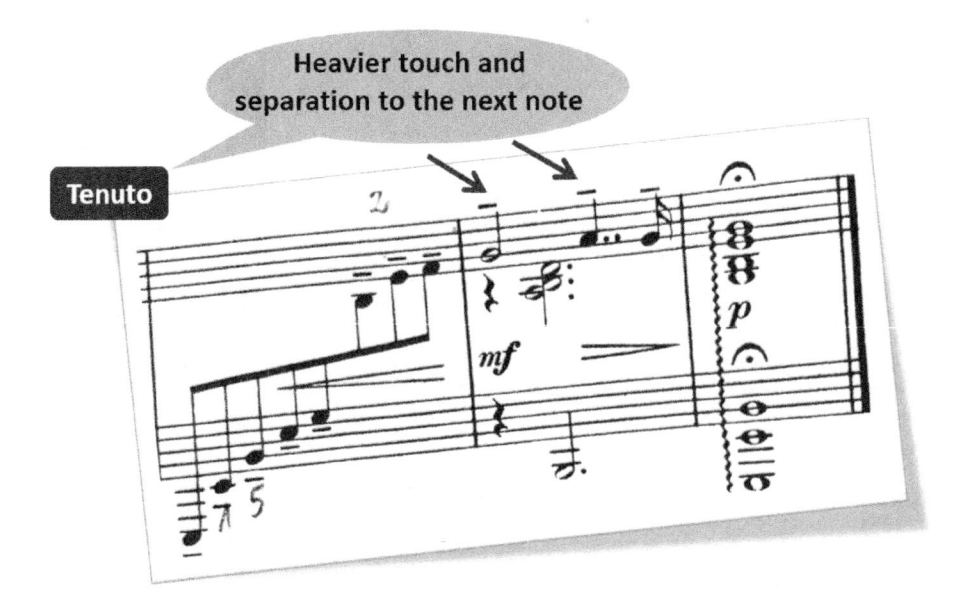

Sforzando

The note should be given an emphasis to bring it out of a musical phrase.

Marcato

Also known as martellato or *martelé*, is a type of sharp accent associated with string playing. The bow is placed on the string and then released quickly and explosively.

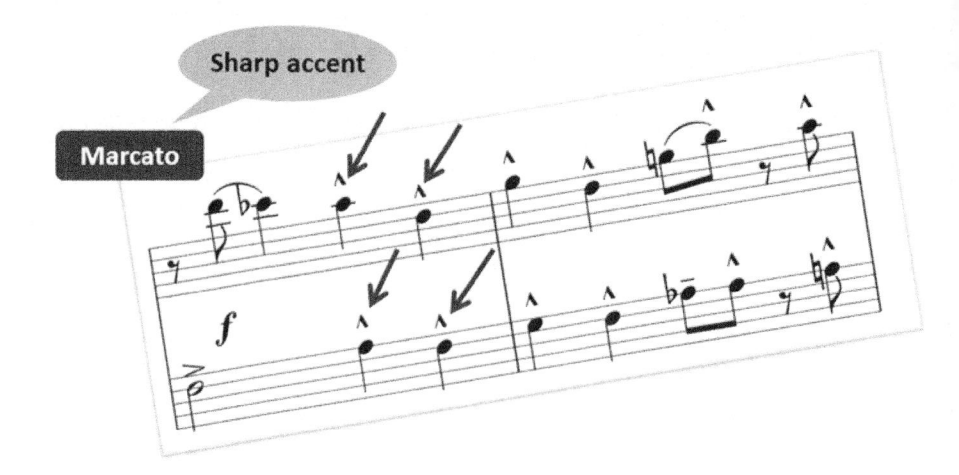

Legato-staccato

Dots inside a slur mean that the notes should be slightly separated (semi-staccato), but less separated than notes with ordinary staccato dots.

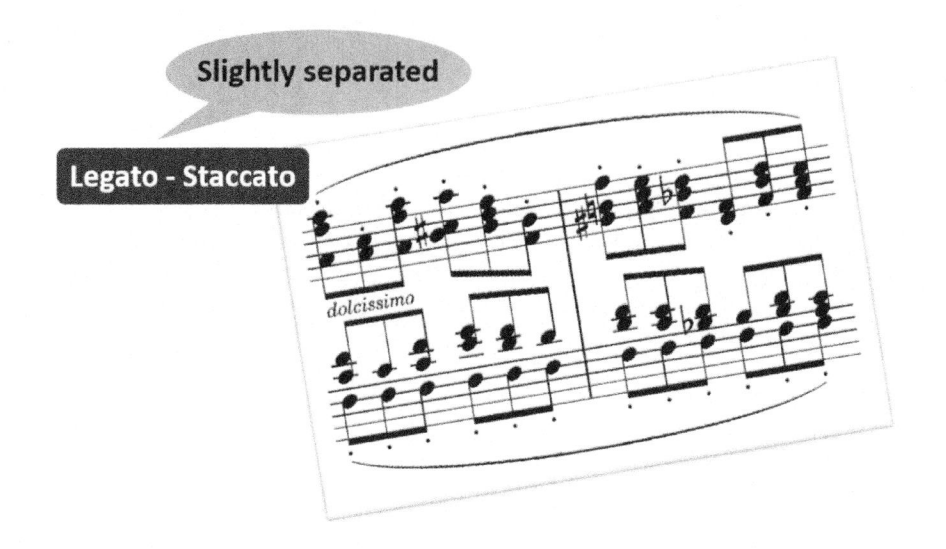

Staccatissimo

A wedge sign indicates a super-staccato. The note is to be played as briefly as possible and perhaps accented as well.

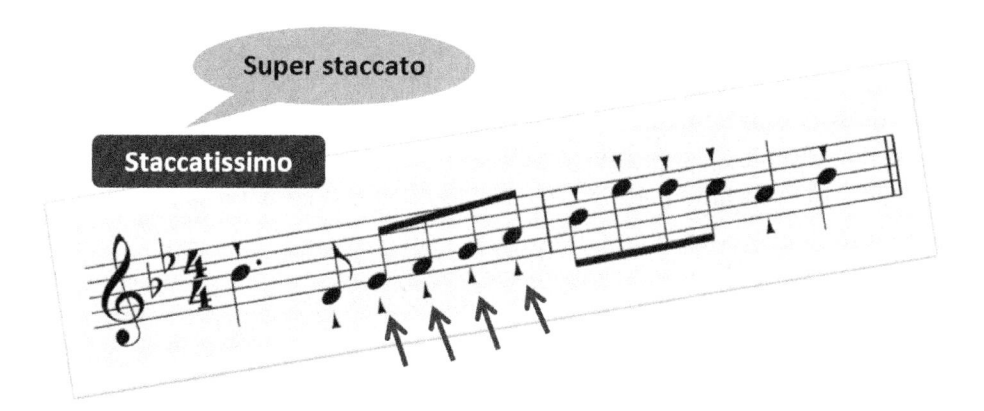

Repeat Marks

Repeats are frequent in music, but there are different ways to represent them depending on how long the repeated section should be.

Repeat Signs

The most basic is the double bar line with two dots. When you see it, you should replay the music either from the beginning of the piece, or from the place where there is another double bar line with the dots facing the right side.

First and second time bar

Play up to the place where you see the repeat sign. Then go back to the beginning but when reaching the end, skip the bar marked as 'first' and play the one marked as 'second'.

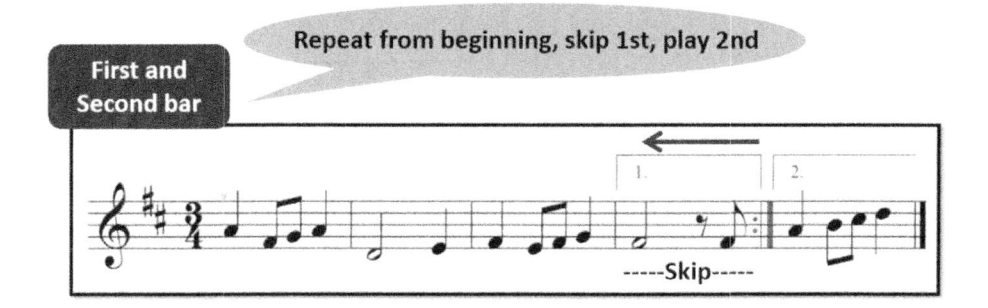

Da Capo al Fine

Da Capo al Fine is usually found at the end of a section or piece. In Italian capo means head, which also refers to the top of something, and Fine is the end.

When there is a Da Capo al Fine in a piece, we need to play again from the top of the piece and finish the performance where we see the Fine.

Dal Segno

Dal Segno is the repeat sign that takes us to replay from a specific place throughout the piece. When we see the letters D.S., we need to replay from the place where the S is written.

Expression Terms

There are many terms to **suggest certain mood or spirit** to be applied to the music. They are usually written below the music. In this level, you will need to know:

Cantabile

In Italian, it means singing and indicates to play with a singing tone and style.

Dolce

The Italian musical term *dolce* literally means sweet. It is an indication to play in a tender, adoring manner; **sweetly with a light touch**.

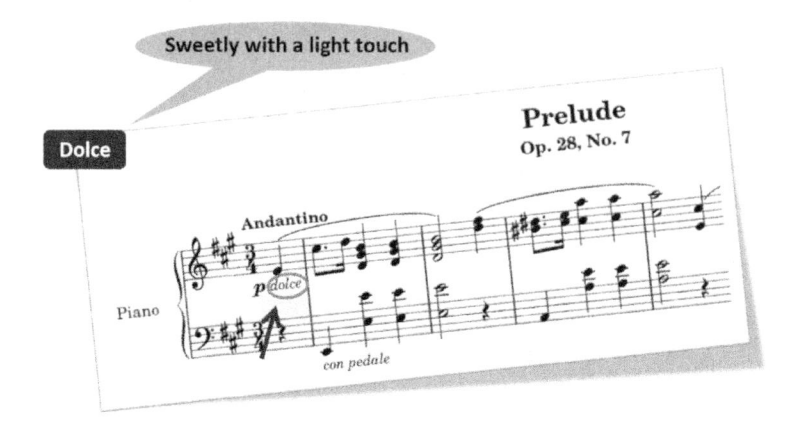

Espressivo

Giocoso

Playful, merry.

Grazioso

Maestoso

Majestic

Other signs and terms

Octave

Other signs that you should also understand are the octave higher and lower. They facilitate sight reading, especially when the notes get so high or low that would need many ledger lines above or below the stave.

The 8va sign written above the stave represents to play the excerpt an octave higher.

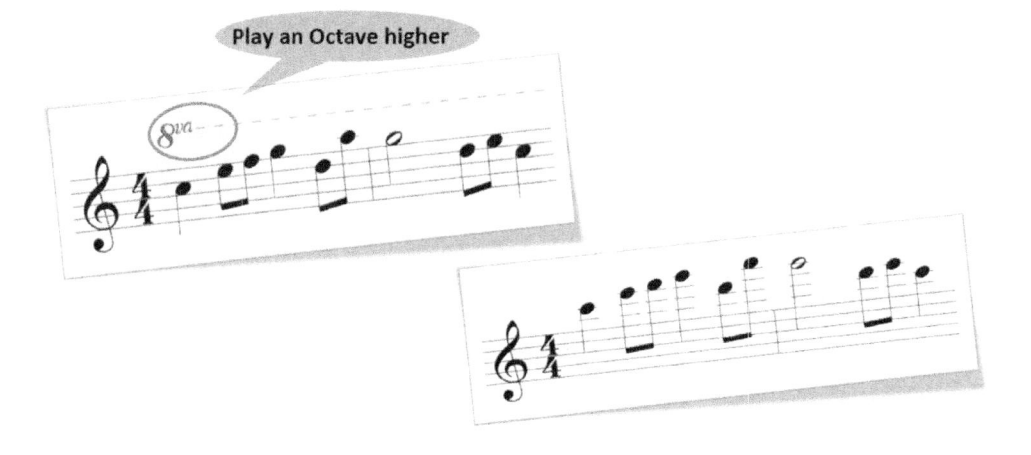

On the other hand, if the sign is written below the stave, it represents to play the excerpt an octave lower.

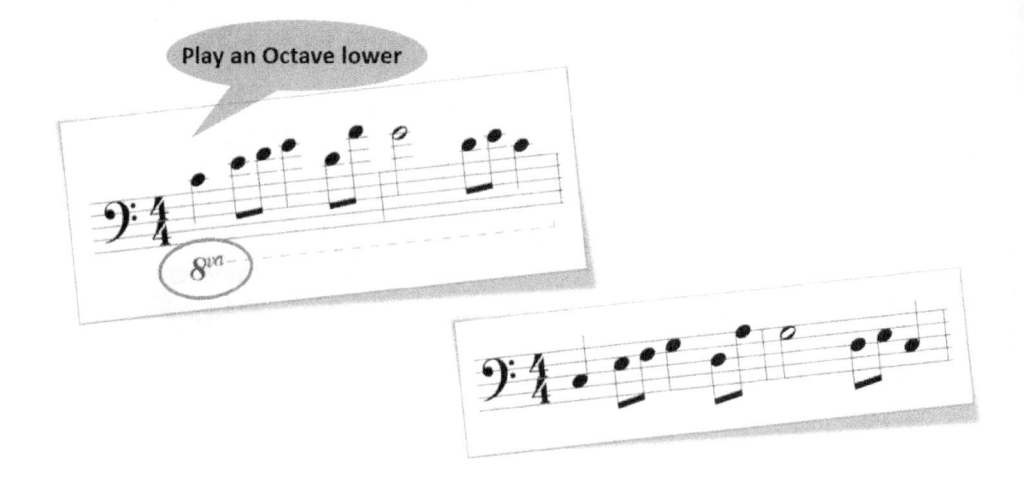

Fermata

The fermata is a sign formed by a little curved line with a dot underneath to represent a prolonged note. It is also common to find them above a rest for the same effect.

For example, this crotchet should last some more time than one beat.

Other terms

A: In Italian, it means "at, to, by, for, in, in the style of"

AL, ALLA: "to the, in the manner of". For example, *alla marcia* means "in the style of a march"

ASSAI: Means "very". Normally used next to another term, for example, *allegro assai* means very quick.

CON, COL: With

E, ED: And

MA: But

MENO: Less

MOLTO: Very, much

MOSSO, MOTO: Means movement. Normally used next to another term, for example, *meno mosso* means slower, *con moto* means with movement.

NON: Not

PIÙ: MORE

SENZA: WITHOUT

SIMILE OR SIM: In the same way

TROPPO: Too much.

NON TROPPO: NOT too much

Musical Vocabulary

ACCOMPANIMENT: Backing. The part that complements a tune.

Am: In relation to chord symbols, it means A minor. It may also appear as Ami, Amin, A-

NATURAL MINOR SCALE: may rarely be called Aeolian mode.

PLAYER: musician, performer, interpret

SHAPE: In relation to the shape of a tune, it relates to its contour, its movements up and down.

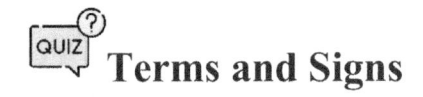

Terms and Signs

https://forms.gle/xtZWWGcCSwYJS1uk6

Music in Context

https://forms.gle/FuSm83eF37y2WVyY7

Mock Test

https://forms.gle/NfsUJhFcANQWsbCu7

From zero to Grade 2

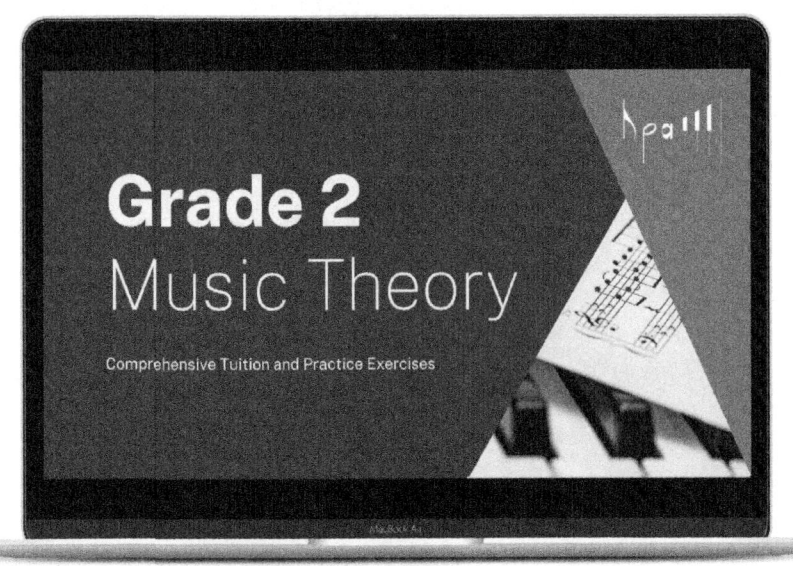

Video Course

at Hampsteadpianoacademy.com

Printed in Great Britain
by Amazon